UNDER THE SUN

UNDER THE SUN
A BLACK JOURNALIST'S JOURNEY

HAROLD JACKSON

THE UNIVERSITY OF ALABAMA PRESS
Tuscaloosa

The University of Alabama Press
Tuscaloosa, Alabama 35487–0380
uapress.ua.edu

Copyright © 2025 by Harold Jackson
All rights reserved.

Inquiries about reproducing material from this work should be addressed to the University of Alabama Press.

Typeface: Garamond Premier Pro

Cover image: Harold Jackson (*right*) interviewing Democratic presidential candidate Barack Obama, April 14, 2008; photography by Elizabeth Robertson, courtesy of the *Philadelphia Inquirer*.

Cover design: Lori Lynch

Excerpt from the editorial "The Cheap Date" by Harold Jackson, *The Birmingham News*, August 27, 1990, published by permission of the Alabama Media Group | The Birmingham News © 1990.

Excerpt from the commentary "When it comes to race, The *Inquirer* may be trying to improve," by Harold Jackson, *Philadelphia Inquirer*, March 21, 2022, published by permission of the Philadelphia Inquirer © 2022.

Cataloging-in-Publication data is available from the Library of Congress.
ISBN: 978-0-8173-2236-6 (cloth)
ISBN: 978-0-8173-6208-9 (paper)
E-ISBN: 978-0-8173-9561-2

TO LEWIS, JANYE, ANTHONY, AND CALVIN JACKSON.
I WILL SEE YOU AGAIN.

CONTENTS

Preface ix

Acknowledgments xi

1. Don't Hide Your Truth   1
2. Life in the Brickyard   3
3. Don't Use Segregation as an Excuse   12
4. Racism Doesn't Spare Children   15
5. Battleground Birmingham   19
6. Sometimes Evil Leads to Good   24
7. Daddy's Stroke Changed Everything   26
8. Finding Strength in Our Church   30
9. High School Can Be Scary   33
10. Introduction to Journalism   36
11. "We Don't Want to Integrate"   39
12. Couldn't Shake George Wallace's Hand   46
13. Time to Get a Real Job   50
14. Newsrooms Were Smoky and Loud   53
15. "Livin' la Vida Loca" in the Projects   59
16. Stepping into Matrimony   73
17. Can't Feed a Family on Peanuts   77

CONTENTS

18. Every Day's a Challenge in Philly   83
19. Weren't Trying to Win a Pulitzer   88
20. Leaving Birmingham Again   94
21. Never Asked Calvin if He Was Gay   101
22. Love Is Medicine   104
23. The Secrets We Keep   109
24. Living in Fear of Being Fired   111
25. Filling the Gaps in Mama's Story   114
26. Avoiding the Noose-Strangling Newspapers   120
27. Abroad in Ethiopia and China   125
28. Need to Get Out of Philly, Again   130
29. Lost Faith in My Church, Not God   133
30. Final Landing Spot, Houston   138
31. Paid to Write What I Believe   141
32. Life under the Sun   148
Epilogue   154
Index   157

Photographs follow page 64

PREFACE

Did I ever think I would become a Pulitzer Prize–winning journalist when I was growing up in a Birmingham, Alabama, housing project during the 1950s and '60s? No. It wasn't that I thought such a lofty goal was impossible for a Black boy in the segregated South. My teachers never dwelled on race being an obstacle to any goal. Instead, we were taught Black children could achieve anything if we worked hard enough. Still, any career as a writer seemed impractical to someone whose family at times struggled to make ends meet, especially after Daddy died.

It was in high school that I learned being a writer didn't necessarily mean trying to become the next Langston Hughes or James Baldwin. That was when my English teachers introduced me to journalism. I was recruited as a freshman to be on the student newspaper staff and that spring became one of the first Black students in the University of Alabama's summer journalism workshop for high school students.

That was in 1968, a scant five years after Governor George Wallace symbolically "stood in the schoolhouse door" in a vain attempt to keep the university and all public schools in Alabama segregated. My experience during that workshop put me on a path that led to a forty-five-year career as a newspaper reporter and editor.

Living in a dormitory and walking freely on the Alabama campus also allowed me to not just see white people but actually talk to them, work with them, and even think that one day some of them might become my friends. That didn't happen for me at the university in 1968. It was way too early. It took years for me to learn how to maneuver past racial prejudices and other biases that prevent friendships and sometimes hinder a person's career.

PREFACE

Becoming a successful journalist meant learning how to get white people I was interviewing to see past my Blackness and answer my questions. It meant realizing that some situations might require me to adapt not only my natural personality but even my style of clothing. Making those adjustments sometimes reminded me of the sociologist W. E. B. DuBois, who, 150 years ago, said Black people out of necessity live double lives—behaving one way among themselves and quite another around white folks.

Of course, it's not just Black people who choose to live double lives to fit in, to be successful, to make friends, and to be loved.

ACKNOWLEDGMENTS

This book would not have been possible without God and my loving parents, Janye and Lewis Jackson, who devoted themselves completely to me and my four brothers, Anthony, Jeffery, Don, and Calvin. I also thank God for my wife, Denice, who stood with me through pitfalls and pinnacles while being the best mother our children, Dennis and Annette, could ever have. I thank my best friend since childhood, Charles Abron, whose memory, much better than mine, helped me remember events recounted in this book.

I want to thank my first grade teacher, Laura P. Sterling, who, by teaching me to read, put me on a path that led to a writing career. I thank my Ullman High School English teachers, Reva Coleman and Kathryn H. Robinson, whose recommendation led to my becoming one of the first Black participants in the University of Alabama high school journalism workshop. I thank my Baker University journalism professors Beverly Paulson and Richard Lindeborg, whose instruction provided the fundamentals I needed to get my first newspaper job.

For that first job, I thank the late *Birmingham Post-Herald* editor Duard LeGrand. For my second job, with United Press International, I thank Alabama editor Richard Beene. For my third job, with the *Philadelphia Inquirer*, I thank national editor Lois Wark. For my fourth job, with the *Birmingham News*, I thank executive editor Jim Jacobson. For my fifth job, with the *Baltimore Sun*, I thank managing editor Bill Marimow. For my sixth job, again with the *Philadelphia Inquirer*, I thank New Jersey editor Julie Busby. For my seventh job, with the *Houston Chronicle*, I thank editorial page editor Lisa Falkenberg.

I would not have authored my story without being inspired by two mentors now departed from this world who became close friends during my journalism

ACKNOWLEDGMENTS

career, *Philadelphia Inquirer* columnist Acel Moore and *Birmingham News* reporter Ingrid Kindred. I'm sending my thanks to them in heaven.

I also want to thank Texas Southern University journalism professor Michael Berryhill, who read my first draft and told me I had a better story to tell; Paul Delaney, retired *New York Times* senior editor; Jack E. White Jr., former *Time* magazine editor; Ed Mullins, former dean of the College of Communication and Information Sciences at the University of Alabama; Rick Bragg, a UA professor and former *New York Times* reporter; and Wanda Lloyd, former *Montgomery Advertiser* executive editor. They all provided much-appreciated advice.

Lastly, I thank University of Alabama Press editor-in-chief Daniel Waterman, who turned a newspaper writer into a book author. Dan's guidance gave me a better appreciation for what a writer can accomplish when he's not limited to eight hundred words in an opinion column.

UNDER THE SUN

CHAPTER 1

DON'T HIDE YOUR TRUTH

I have seen all the works that are done under the sun; and behold, all is vanity and vexation of spirit.
—Ecclesiastes 1:14

God seems to like catching our attention when we least expect it.

On an otherwise unremarkable summer day in 1996, my phone rang at the *Baltimore Sun*. I was doing some research to write an editorial about a topic I no longer remember, but I will never forget what happened next.

I answered the phone as I usually did—not by reciting my name or the newspaper's but by sounding as if I were lounging in a chair at home. "Hello," I said. "Hello," a man responded before hurriedly reciting a speech he likely had rehearsed many times before dialing my number. "My name is Ricky Marquis. I'm a friend of your brother Calvin."

I immediately felt nervous. Calvin lived three thousand miles away in San Francisco, and none of his friends had ever called me. Something must be wrong. Was he in trouble? Was he sick? None of my fears prepared me for Ricky's next words.

"Calvin doesn't know I'm calling," he said, "but there's something you need to know. Calvin is sick. He's dying. Of AIDS."

The rest of that conversation remains lost in fog. I don't remember how I responded. My cubicle was designed to resemble a small office with just enough room for a desk, file cabinet, and a second chair for visitors, but the partition

CHAPTER 1

walls separating it from the other cubicles were paper thin and didn't extend to the ceiling. Anything I said could be overheard, and I didn't want anyone to hear me if I started crying.

When Ricky finished, I thanked him, sat at my desk for about an hour, and then went home to tell my wife, Denice, what had happened. I wiped tears from my eyes as I drove, not just because Calvin was dying but because the youngest of Lewis and Janye Jackson's five sons had tried to keep the truth that he was gay hidden from his family—fearing they would no longer love him.

CHAPTER 2

LIFE IN THE BRICKYARD

I always felt closet to my youngest brother, Calvin, even though there was a four-year age gap. Calvin was born in 1957; I, 1953; Don, 1952; Jeffery, 1950; and my oldest brother, Anthony, 1946. Our own Jackson Five. Despite our age gap, Calvin and I always seemed more in synch. He wasn't just my brother; he was my friend. We traded insults, told inside jokes, and made up nicknames for some of the colorful characters we grew up around in the Loveman Village housing project. Residents of the dozens of rows of rent-subsidized "garden" apartments called the complex the Brick Yard.

I lived in Loveman Village from the day Mama and Daddy brought me home as a baby from St. Vincent's Hospital in 1953 until Denice and I got married in 1977 and moved into our own home. The Brick Yard changed dramatically during that span, as did housing projects all across America. There weren't as many single-parent families in Loveman Village in the 1950s, and all the "baby daddies" I knew back then were married and had jobs. My daddy drove a delivery truck for R. B. Broyles Furniture Co., while Mama stayed home to cook, clean, and otherwise make sure their five boys were fed, clothed, and where she could find them.

Families in Loveman Village were expected to keep their apartment clean and its premises properly maintained. Push lawn mowers to cut the grass could be checked out at the rental office. Tenants were required to allow periodic inspections of their apartments to ensure proper maintenance of its furnace,

CHAPTER 2

stove, refrigerator, and hot water heater. Complaints about noise or other objectionable behavior could lead to eviction. The area we lived in was typically quiet in the 1950s. Except for the sound of children playing outside, the relative silence was only occasionally broken by pianos being played in one of two apartments: one where Ms. Plant, a gray-haired spinster, taught lessons to children I didn't recognize as being projects residents, and the other was occupied by a family of five, including three daughters, who seemed to take turns at almost any time of the day pounding out the notes to the only song they apparently knew—"Heart and Soul."

By the 1970s, however, both the often disharmonious piano notes and the more tranquil music emanating from Ms. Plant's home were too frequently drowned out by loud stereos playing, people arguing, and sometimes gunshots. That's also when single parenthood became more prevalent in Loveman Village, along with alcoholism, teenage pregnancy, and kids joining gangs and selling dope.

Too many kids I knew stopped believing in a future beyond the borders of the projects. Too many were like Carl, who lived with his mom and sister in an apartment across from ours. I remember how Carl seemed so full of enthusiasm when he graduated high school and went away to college. But less than two years later, he was back home and eventually became just another wino trying to scrounge up change to buy a bottle.

I won't blame the projects for that. I don't know all that was going on in Carl's life, but I do know that too many of us who grew up amid the same challenges that Carl faced made better choices. One role model for me was Frank Horn, an older kid who lived a couple of apartments down from us. Frank joined the Army after high school and in 1966 became one of Birmingham's first Black police officers.

One day when I was sitting on our back porch, I saw Frank get into an argument with two guys we knew who were harassing him for being a cop. Frank was wearing his uniform and went inside his mother's apartment to put away his gun before reappearing, ready to fight. It was two against one, but Frank eventually had the thugs retreating while they were hurling some choice curse words in his direction.

Years later, when I was a reporter, I interviewed Frank, who had become executive director of Birmingham's Partners in Neighborhood Growth (PING) recreational program for low-income youths. I asked Frank to talk about the difficulties of being one of the first Black cops in what Martin Luther King Jr.

and others had called America's most segregated city. Frank said most white officers seemed to be looking for any hint that he would be more "Black" than "Blue." He said he tried to stay true to both his race and his duty as a policeman.

Having stern mothers as children sort of made Frank and me kindred spirits, though we were otherwise nothing alike. Like Mama, Miss Dolly didn't hesitate to use a belt to keep her three sons, Frank, Jesse, and Emmanuel, in line. Mama said Daddy didn't want to whip us because he didn't want us to hate him. That raised all kinds of questions in my mind about Daddy's childhood, but I never asked them. Besides, it wasn't as if Daddy didn't punish us if he felt the crime required it. The sting of his whippings lasted much longer than Mama's did, but we didn't "hate" him or her.

Mama helped us stay out of trouble by minimizing our contact with bad influences when our schoolwork and chores were done. We would play cards, dominoes, checkers, or other games that kept us either inside our apartment or on our or a neighbor's porch. We had toys but sometimes devised our own, like the dozens of soda pop bottle tops we collected and grouped by color, pretending they were armies waging war on our bedroom floor.

Calvin and I would sometimes use toys to produce our versions of soap operas like *Search for Tomorrow* and *Guiding Light* that Mama watched on TV. Toy soldiers and other action figures served as the male protagonists in our dramas, but there were no dolls in our house to perform the female roles. No problem. Calvin would use a pocketknife to carefully roll down the bark on sticks to resemble long hair. I laughed at his ingenuity but otherwise never gave it much thought. Our soap operas typically ended with a murder or brawl, and then we would look for something else to do, most likely read a book.

My brothers and I were avid readers and thought nothing of walking the mile to the library branch that served Titusville, a Black community in southwest Birmingham. The attentive librarians seemed to know every child. Mrs. Blackburn, the head librarian, would patiently assist us in finding the right book or periodical for our homework or in looking for something fun to read. My brothers and I would check out dozens of books during the library's annual summer reading program and earn certificates with gold or silver stars for every level of achievement.

The library was practically next door to the church we attended, Westminster Presbyterian, with only one house between the two buildings. Westminster's congregation was small, with fewer than 150 members. Most were middle class, but they all seemed rich to projects dwellers like my family. My

CHAPTER 2

big brother Anthony first visited Westminster at the invitation of its pastor, the Reverend John Rice, who was also his guidance counselor at Ullman High School.

Ullman students liked "the Rev's" church, whose vibrant youth fellowship program for teenagers was run by Julia Emma Smith, an elementary school art teacher. "Westminster was a happening place"—that was what I wrote in a 2002 column for the *Philadelphia Inquirer* that recalled my childhood. "Rev would show movies, organize games, even hold parties in the church annex and allow us to dance. You bet the Baptists wouldn't do that."

Who knew then that Rev. Rice's daughter, Condoleezza, would grow up to become the US secretary of state in 2005 for President George W. Bush? Condoleezza and I barely knew each other as children, but she does mention me in her 2010 memoir, *Extraordinary, Ordinary People*, as "a Youth Fellowship kid from the Village" who "credited Daddy for laying the spiritual foundation for his life." My spiritual growth continued after the Rice family moved to Denver in 1968 and the Reverend Clyde Carter became Westminster's pastor.

In a column that I wrote in 2002, after Bush initially made her his national security advisor, I recalled what I thought of Condoleezza when she was a little girl. "I was the knucklehead trying not laugh in my pew at a buddy's jokes; Condoleezza was the no-nonsense little girl in matching dress and anklets who wouldn't waste the effort to look our way," I said. "At that age, who gives a darn about girls anyway, especially one so smart she played piano for the adult choir?"

My family became members of Westminster in 1964. Before that we didn't go to church regularly but sometimes attended vacation Bible school classes at nearby churches. Sometimes we walked to the occasional revivals held outdoors in front of a little convenience store near our apartment. Loveman Village residents mostly bought sundries, snacks, and sodas from the store, which we called the "stand." It was operated by Mr. Toby, who was legally blind but would put bills close to his eyes to determine their denomination or, presumably, to see if they were counterfeit.

Mama was raised Baptist but joined her sons in becoming a Presbyterian after we became members of Westminster. Daddy visited a few times but never became a member. Maybe he felt self-conscious among the teachers and other professionals in the congregation while our family lived in the projects. I was just happy anytime Daddy came to church. His rare appearances were enough to assure me Daddy was a believer in Christ and that I would see him in heaven.

Sundays after church were usually peaceful, but even on the Lord's day five boys jockeying for personal space in a small apartment can lead to territorial disputes that quickly escalate from shouting to shoving and—if Mama was too late to intervene—trading licks. Mama encouraged us to avoid potential disciplinary action by staking out a quiet nook in our three-bedroom apartment and curling up alone with a book.

Of course, we also could watch TV, which was much easier in those days before cable and streaming when there were only three network choices (ABC, CBS, or NBC). We got our first television around 1957, when I was four. Once we got a TV, it was hard to think of ever being without one. A rabbit-ears antenna sitting atop our small black-and-white set usually ensured decent reception.

Mama liked soap operas and Daddy liked boxing and baseball, but their sons' tastes ranged from cartoons such as *Huckleberry Hound* and *Mighty Mouse*, to fictional cowboys such as Roy Rogers and Hopalong Cassidy, to any scary movie featuring Frankenstein, Dracula, or Wolfman, to science fiction cult classics including *Them*, *The Day the Earth Stood Still*, *Forbidden Planet*, and *X the Unknown*.

Of course, the genre didn't matter if anyone Black unexpectedly appeared on our TV screen. Those occasions were so rare in the 1960s that whoever was watching made sure to shout out to everyone else in the house so they wouldn't miss it. Black performers typically appeared on popular variety shows like *The Ed Sullivan Show* and *The Rosemary Clooney Show*, including Nat King Cole, Sammy Davis Jr., Lena Horne, Eartha Kitt, Pearl Bailey, and Louis Armstrong. Tap dancer "Peg Leg" Bates and comedian "Moms" Mabley appeared less often. Any Black person's appearance on TV was guaranteed to increase that show's Black audience.

Even as children, we understood the importance of those moments, which helped provide hope to our parents that one day white people would treat Black people as their equals beyond a TV stage. We were proud not only of the Black performers' talent but of their dress, decorum, and speech. We believed their appearances on TV could help to dispel the negative stereotypes that white people used as excuses to discriminate.

Compare that with the casual acceptance by today's Black TV audiences of Black entertainers whose popularity is in large part based on their dressing,

CHAPTER 2

speaking, and acting like stereotypes of the street thugs that Black people in the 1960s begged white people to understand were not representative of our people.

Even I eventually became a fan of some rap music, but I hate that too many of its most successful artists, male and female, seem to promote violence, larceny, and misogyny. Older, richer rappers like Jay-Z, LL Cool J, Ludacris, Ice-T, and Ice Cube have toned down that persona to make more money by appealing to wider audiences. But the genre remains basically unchanged, as even suburban white kids try to act like Black "gangstas."

Some popular Black performers when I was a child similarly promoted negative stereotypes, including actors like Stepin Fetchit and Mantan Moreland, who typically played slow-witted, slow-talking, slow-moving servants in movies we watched on TV. More prominent were the cast members of the TV series *Amos 'n' Andy*, which centered around the get-rich-quick schemes of a conniving lawyer whose exploits suggested all Black people were either crooks or dolts.

My family and others acted like the proverbial man who savors the meat he's chewing while spitting out its bones and watched *Amos 'n' Andy* despite its faults. We were that hungry to see people who looked like us and talked like us in TV roles that didn't require them to dress like a maid or butler and serve white people. It would have been easy to write *Amos 'n' Andy*'s comedic routines so they exemplified human frailty, regardless of race, but that would have implied an equality that the show's producers apparently didn't want to risk presenting.

As much as I am embarrassed to say I enjoyed watching *Amos 'n' Andy*, I also have to admit my brothers and I were also big fans of *The Gray Ghost*, a TV show that, when we were quite young, ran from 1957 to 1958. We saw it only as an adventure series depicting the exploits of a dashing calvary officer who wielded a sword as well as a pistol. It never dawned on us that the dashing officer was a Confederate soldier raising his weapons against Union troops fighting to free slaves who looked like us.

The series was based on the true story of Major John Singleton Mosby, a Virginian in the Confederate army whose stealth earned him the nickname "Gray Ghost." It was years after reruns of the show stopped that I realized I had been idolizing the fictional depiction of a real person who had fought to keep my ancestors enslaved. The brief popularity of that show suggests the pervasiveness of the post-Civil War effort to elevate traitors to hero status even one hundred years later. No wonder it took decades to begin removing the statues of Confederate generals from public squares. No wonder it's still hard to get some "patriotic" Americans to reject the lie those statues promoted.

I watched so much TV as a child that my classmates at Baker University in Kansas noticed my lack of a Southern drawl. "Why don't you talk like Senora?" they asked. Senora Todd was another Black student who coincidentally was also from Birmingham. I would smile and say I learned to talk watching TV, which was close to being true. I never purposely mimicked the actors I watched as a child, but I may have inadvertently adopted some of their pronunciations and idioms.

Most of the students at Baker were Midwesterners. But fellow Southerners long before that had similarly taken note of my speech. Some of the kids in the Birmingham projects where I grew up accused me of "talking proper," a euphemism for "talking white." Ironically, some white friends I worked with after college also accused me of not talking like the Black people they knew.

Whenever that happened, I was reminded of sociologist W. E. B. DuBois's assessment in an 1897 article for the *Atlantic* that Black people live double lives. "One feels his two-ness—an American, a Negro; two souls, two thoughts, two unreconciled strivings; two warring ideals in one dark body, whose dogged strength alone keeps it from being torn asunder."

Just because we liked to watch TV didn't mean my brothers and I spent most of our free time inside the house. Maybe we would have if we'd had today's electronic toys and devices. But we enjoyed playing outdoors with our friends. Mama liked that too. Our playing outside made it easier for her to keep a clean house. If you add it up, we probably spent more time outdoors than indoors—riding bikes, roller-skating, playing marbles, hide-and-seek, tag, or a game we invented. We liked pretending to be cops and robbers or cowboys and Indians so we could buckle up our side holsters, break out our cap guns, and shoot it out.

Mostly, I played with my brothers and other boys who lived nearby, but sometimes I would ride my tricycle or walk to the end of our apartment unit to play "house" with June and Connie Cooper, two cute sisters about a year or so younger than me. They would get out their toy cups and saucers and plates, and we would pretend to eat dinner. Other times, I was content to sit alone on our front porch and watch ants haul their cargoes of crumbs to their nests with deliberate speed. I even thought about becoming an entomologist when I was old enough to understand what that meant. But studying insects never became my vocation.

CHAPTER 2

The one big drawback to playing outdoors is knowing eventually you will have to go inside. Worse was knowing that bedtime for the Jackson boys typically came sooner than it did for our friends, even during the summer, when the sun didn't set until after eight o'clock. It didn't matter that school was out; Mama's dictum was always early to bed, early to rise. Knowing we were in bed while they were still playing, our friends would laugh and yell up to our open bedroom window for us to come play tag. After a while, their taunts became a discordant lullaby as I drifted into sleep.

When we weren't playing outside, watching TV, or reading, the Jackson brothers liked to debate, though it might be more accurate to call it arguing, since no rules were applied. Mama wasn't about to allow any physical combat among her five boys, either inside the house or out. So verbal jousts became our substitute. Lacking a judge to tally points meant victory could be claimed by whoever managed to get the last word. Over the years I became so adept at "debating" that my friends in elementary school said I should become a lawyer.

The closest I ever got to a real fight was in the ninth grade. Many of Ullman High School's varsity football players had enrolled in the same seventh-period gym class that I was in so they could go directly from class to practice. Apparently trying to impress the upperclassmen during an unsupervised game of touch football, Alvin Vanhorn, another freshman, started boasting that he was going to hit me so hard I would see stars. I ignored Alvin until he decided to add gusto to his threats by getting in my face and screaming them. Without thinking, I socked him in the jaw.

"What you do that for?" shouted Alvin, but he retreated. The varsity football players snickered, gym class went on, and I learned an important lesson. Most bullies are, to use Shakespeare's words, but in a different context, "full of sound and fury. Signifying nothing."

My oratory prowess may have helped me avoid a beating by other potential antagonists but proved useless in deterring Mama from exacting corporal punishment when she felt my behavior warranted it. My most lasting memory of that occurred when I was about eleven years old and dared Calvin, who was seven, to step on the pocketknife I was playing with while sitting on our hallway stairs. It was never Calvin's nature to retreat from a challenge, but I thought I could pull the knife away before he stepped on it. I didn't. He stepped on the blade. His foot was cut. He bled.

"What's wrong with you?" I shouted as Calvin, who seemed dumbfounded, merely stared at his bleeding foot. The panic in my voice immediately brought Mama to the scene, who first tended to Calvin's wound before coming back to me, still sitting on the steps, already weeping in anticipation of what I knew was coming. Even now I think Mama should have whipped Calvin for being not just obstinate but dumb enough to step on a knife. But I was the dummy for thinking he wouldn't do it.

That was Calvin. Had Mama and Daddy given him a middle name, which they didn't, "Adamant" would have been a good choice. Calvin never backed down. I'm sure my backside hurt more than his foot after Mama got through with me. Regardless, the next day we were back to being friends. We didn't talk about his foot, the knife, or anything else that might have diminished our friendship. No wonder we never talked about a truth that, even as his death approached, Calvin tried to keep secret.

CHAPTER 3

DON'T USE SEGREGATION AS AN EXCUSE

Kindergarten wasn't required in Alabama in 1959, so my brothers and I never went. That meant I was behind many of my classmates when I started first grade at Center Street Elementary School. My teacher, Laura P. Sterling, put me in the Group Four reading group for children who couldn't read, which was embarrassing. I thought she might as well have put a dunce cap on my head. But before the school year ended, I was in Group One. Reading came easy to me once I learned my ABCs. In fact, school seemed easy in almost every way.

That's not a commentary on the academic rigor at Center Street, which I attended through eighth grade. I'm criticizing myself for becoming satisfied with doing just enough to get good grades. They could have been even better had I worked harder, which is what I was raised to do. My parents stressed to their five sons that we should always do our best, no matter the task, even if it was sweeping the floor. I brought home good report cards, but some Bs could have been As.

My lack of motivation can't be blamed on my teachers, or on Center Street's principal, Roscoe Sheehy. They never used the glaring inequities within Birmingham's segregated school system as an excuse for students not to excel. I called Mr. Sheehy a "tyrant" in a 1995 *Baltimore Evening Sun* article, but I meant it in a good way. "He was the best," I said. "But he probably wouldn't have held his job long today."

The six-foot-plus, athletically built man was a no-nonsense type of guy. He never let hurting anyone's feelings stand in his way. Students hated him. And they loved him. You got the sense that the teachers felt the same way." One day during an afterschool sock-hop, where older kids took off their shoes to dance and younger ones did the same to playfully slide across the gym's hardwood floor, Mr. Sheehy suddenly appeared and angrily grabbed the PA system microphone.

He gruffly ordered our school's janitor to immediately open all the gym's windows and doors and began berating his mostly preteen audience for our poor hygiene, even suggesting that better parents wouldn't have sent us to school without deodorant.

That wouldn't happen today, but Black parents in the 1960s understood what principals like Sheehy were trying to do. They knew the harshness of his statements was meant to help their children understand they couldn't provide bigoted white people with any additional excuse to consider them inferior. It wasn't enough to be smart or talented; we had to smell like someone that white folks might tolerate.

Mr. Sheehy didn't mind hurting Black children's feelings to teach us that lesson, but not even his outbursts motivated me to do more academically. It didn't help that my grades were better than any of the other boys' in my classes. I didn't care about the girls. The smartest students in my classes from first through the eighth grades were Clara Frierson, Shandra Jackson, and Alicia Springer, whose father, John Springer, taught both band and science at Center Street.

Mr. Springer once threw a ball of string at me for talking in class when I was in the seventh grade. The class laughed, but I was horrified, imagining Mama's reaction if she ever heard about my conduct. Fortunately, Mr. Springer was satisfied with getting my attention. But later that same school year, I was punished by Elisha Blissett, who succeeded Mr. Sheehy after he became Ullman High School's principal.

Mr. Blissett heard our noisy class as he approached it to check on our substitute teacher and chose three students to stand outside his office as punishment. I was one of them. How embarrassing it was for me, someone more likely to be caught daydreaming while looking out a window than talking. Thankfully, Mama never heard about that incident either.

The number of teachers with children who attended Center Street may have had an impact on the education we received. Besides Mr. Springer, my first-grade teacher, Mrs. Sterling, and second-grade teacher, Johnnie Mae High, had children at Center Street. Other teachers lived within walking distance of the school, which meant they were neighbors to some of my classmates and friends of their parents. But even those of us who lived in Loveman Village felt a closer connection to our teachers because, unlike many of their counterparts today, they didn't drive home to some far-flung suburb when school was out.

Attending the same elementary school for eight years contributed to my comfort level. Mama and Daddy never questioned my effort because my teachers never gave them reason to worry. But one day, my seventh-grade geography teacher called me out. Jezeree Lewis was a tall woman with a square jaw, so students nicknamed her "Chuck Connors," after the pro basketball player-turned-actor who starred in *The Rifleman*, a popular TV Western. Mrs. Lewis told me I had too much potential to waste. "I know you can do better, Harold."

Those words almost made me cry. Her genuine concern touched me. Not only did I not want to disappoint my parents, but I also didn't want to disappoint Mrs. Lewis. Her taking the time to encourage me motivated me to work harder, but I still didn't get an academic award when my eight-grade class graduated in 1967. In fact, no boy received an academic award, which made me feel like I had let my entire gender down.

I vowed to do better in high school, but distractions not just at home but in Birmingham as a whole made that more difficult. The school system began a painful but necessary transition that ended segregation and allowed students to learn that much of what we had been told about our Black or white counterparts wasn't even close to the truth.

CHAPTER 4

RACISM DOESN'T SPARE CHILDREN

One unintentional benefit of segregation was that it sheltered most Black children from the indignities our parents routinely faced every day. A Black child living in the Deep South before integration might go an entire day, morning to night, without ever seeing a white person anywhere except on TV. Conversely, it was damn near impossible for our parents to avoid some level of interaction with white people, either while working, shopping, or simply walking down a downtown street.

I didn't always recognize segregation when I was a child. When I was five years old, Mama had to scramble to find an alley behind a downtown department store one day so I could urinate. I had no idea our emergency was due to the store's refusal to allow me to use their bathrooms—the same store that took our money to buy socks and shoes. I didn't know that letting me use a "white" toilet was against the law. I had no idea that it wasn't always a choice when my brothers and I rode with our parents in the back of city buses.

That was in the 1960s, when Birmingham was considered the most segregated city in America. It was quite a distinction for a town that didn't exist during the Civil War but nevertheless clung to the racial biases of that age as if it had birthed them. Birmingham was founded in 1871 by Northern industrialists who hoped the area's abundant coal and iron ore would make it the Pittsburgh of the South. Those men then exploited the South's racism to keep their

CHAPTER 4

white and black workers in the coal mines and steel mills from finding common ground by unionizing.

The previously failed efforts of Birmingham's Black community to end segregation in the city were revived in 1955 after the US Supreme Court's *Brown v. Board of Education* decision. The fight was led by the Reverend Fred Shuttlesworth, who, with the Reverend Ed Garner, founded the Alabama Christian Movement for Human Rights after the NAACP was banned in Alabama.

I interviewed Shuttlesworth for a *Birmingham News* column in 1993. People started calling him "Crazy Fred" in the 1950s for not letting beatings and bomb threats deter him from his goal of integrating Birmingham. But after years of protests that resulted in little or no progress, he knew he needed help from outside the city.

Needing someone to spark greater participation by the city's Black establishment, especially his fellow ministers, Shuttlesworth reached out to the Reverend Martin Luther King Jr. in 1963. King eagerly accepted the invitation. He needed a victory to match the successful Montgomery bus boycott that he'd led six years earlier. Having moved back to his hometown of Atlanta to be co-pastor of his father's church, King saw an opportunity in Birmingham to resuscitate his national civil rights campaign.

King, Shuttlesworth, and other strategists decided to undermine Birmingham's aggressive campaign to outgrow Atlanta and become the Southeast's economic powerhouse by staging daily marches designed to generate negative news coverage of Alabama's largest city. They knew they could count on Birmingham's racist police commissioner, Eugene "Bull" Connor, to respond brutally to demonstrations.

The plan's success was ensured when they later decided to ask children to march. One of the youngest marchers arrested was Audrey Faye Hendricks, a nine-year-old fourth-grade classmate of mine who spent seven days in jail. Audrey was a friendly, talkative child, but she didn't make much of an impression on me. When you're nine you don't pay much attention to girls, period.

It was years later when I read *Freedom's Children* by Ellen Levine that I learned Audrey's mother had helped plan the daily marches as assistant secretary of the Alabama Christian Movement for Civil Rights. It had to be hard for her to see her child taken to jail. Audrey's parents were activists, but you didn't have to march to know that "separate but equal" was a lie that must die.

The world was outraged by TV news coverage of Black men, women, and children trying to avoid snarling police dogs and blasts of water being shot like cannon balls from firemen's hoses. The progressive image that Birmingham's business community leaders sought for their so-called Magic City was eclipsed by newspaper photos of children in their Sunday best church clothes being hauled off to jail by Connor's dragoons.

Two older boys on bikes tried to talk my brother Don and me into joining the protests when we were walking to school one day. They said Center Street and other Black schools were being boycotted by students so they could march with King. I immediately thought that if the teenage recruiters knew our parents, they would also know no excuse was good enough for us to skip school without their permission. Neither Mama nor Daddy went to college, but they were determined that their sons would. Don and I shook our heads no and kept walking.

I usually walked to school with Don, but going home he typically walked with his classmates and I walked with my best friend, Charles Abron, who also lived in Loveman Village but in another part of the sprawling complex with low-slung buildings, which made it hard for six-year-olds to routinely play at each other's homes. I learned some valuable life lessons walking home with Charles, including what not to do when confronted by a bully. Actually, Mama taught me that lesson, but Charles was there when she did.

One day we were taking our usual shortcut home from school with Ben, another first grader who also lived in the projects. We cut through a wooded area whose tall pine trees and dense bushes were vestiges of what the area looked like before our housing project was developed in the 1950s. Separate groups of mainly boys often lingered in the woods on the way home from school. We cleared spots where we could sit, tell jokes, or retreat to more secluded areas to relieve ourselves.

The three of us had just come out of the woods when I apparently said something Ben didn't like. Or maybe he just felt like picking on me, which frightened me because, though Ben might have been a first grader too, he was a half-foot taller than both Charles and me and had the muscle mass to match. Not knowing what I had done or said to agitate Ben, I was caught off guard when out of the blue he kicked me in the butt. Maybe because I could see the apartment where I lived, I started crying—loudly.

Charles and Ben just stared at me, but Mama, apparently awaiting my arrival either at our front door or near an open window, heard a child crying and within minutes was by my side—which I soon regretted. Never glancing once at Ben or Charles, she commanded me to "get on home!" Once inside, Mama

CHAPTER 4

closed the door, looked me in the eye, and said, "Don't you ever let anybody hit you without hitting back!"

So, I thought but never said aloud, Mama's no-fighting rule applied only to my brothers and me hitting each other. I never forgot that but also learned over the years that "hitting back" doesn't have to be physical.

The woods provided the setting for another important lesson I learned as a third grader. I was walking to school one cold day with a group of four or five boys from the projects. We reached a shallow creek that was a bit higher after recent rains and covered by a thin layer of ice veiling the large stones we typically used to cross to the other side. We needed to either jump about three feet to land on the other side of the stream or walk the long way to school, which would leave little time to play outside before the bell rang for classes to begin.

The other boys rather quickly made up their minds to jump. But, not being able to see what was below the thin ice, I didn't feel as confident. I quietly watched as each of my friends, one by one, ran up to the ice-covered water's edge before hurling themselves with a courage-inducing shout to the other side. Finally, it was my turn. "Jump! Jump! Jump!" they shouted, urgently pointing out that if I didn't hurry up, we wouldn't make it to school before the bell rang.

Finally, unable to put it off any longer and not wanting to be labeled a wimp, I closed my eyes, took a tentative first step, then what was more of a hop than a leap, and landed well short of my intended target. The thin ice cracked as soon as my feet hit it, and suddenly I was knee-deep in freezing water. My "friends" couldn't laugh any harder if they tried. I dared not return home and face Mama, so I walked to school. Fortunately, God spared me the indignity of catching pneumonia, and luckily my school kept a stash of cast-off clothes for such emergencies.

I had to tell Mama what had happened when I came home wearing different clothes, but she didn't get angry. Instead, I was ordered to quickly change clothes so she could wash and dry what I wore home and send them back to school.

If Mama was embarrassed by my having to wear some other child's discarded clothes, she never said it. Maybe she thought it was enough that I learned something from the experience. And I did. I learned from my failed leap across an icy stream that in life every challenge requires preparation. When you need to jump, decide where you want to land, how much effort is required, and if you have the guts to make the leap.

CHAPTER 5

BATTLEGROUND BIRMINGHAM

Birmingham's 1963 civil rights demonstrations ended that spring when its major department stores, Pizitz, Loveman's, and others grudgingly agreed to hire Black salesclerks and integrate their lunch counters, fitting rooms, and restrooms. As modest as those concessions were, they made the Ku Klux Klan so angry it bombed the Gaston Motel, which was where the Reverend Martin Luther King Jr. had stayed when he was planning the daily marches from nearby Kelly Ingram Park.

King had already returned to Atlanta when the motel was bombed, but that didn't stop the Klan from pursuing its intimidation campaign. It set off another bomb outside the home of King's brother, the Reverend A. D. King, who lived in Birmingham. Again, no one was seriously injured, but the city remained on edge.

At least eight suspected Klan bombings occurred in Birmingham after the settlement in May that ended the civil rights demonstrations. Twice during that period bombs exploded at the home of civil rights attorney Arthur Shores, who in 1968 became the first Black member of the Birmingham City Council.

A close encounter I had that summer taught me children aren't exempt from racists who decide to spit their venom. Mama had sent me to the A&P supermarket less than a mile from our home because the small grocery store closer to our home didn't have the coffee she wanted. A&P was a national chain with its own brand, Eight O' Clock Coffee, which is still sold in stores

CHAPTER 5

across America, even though A&P, after several bankruptcies, went out of business in 2016.

With cash in my pocket to buy coffee, I was standing at the intersection where the A&P was located, waiting for the traffic light to change. When it did, I put my foot out but quickly withdrew it just as an old pickup truck that must have run the light sped past me. "Nigger! Nigger! Nigger!" yelled three white children holding onto the moving truck's sides while standing in its cargo bed. The children looked to be from about six to eleven years old, two boys wearing jeans and a pigtailed girl in a dress, laughing at my astonished reaction.

My first thought was how close I had come to death. The truck missed me only by a second or two. I started blaming myself for not being more careful. Mama trusted me at age nine to run this errand because I knew better than to cross a street without looking both ways. I calmed down, crossed the street to the A&P when it was safe, bought the coffee, and went home. I never mentioned the incident to Mama or Daddy, still thinking I may have been at fault. Besides, what could they do about it?

The more I thought about it, though, the more I realized my carelessness wasn't why those white children spat racist profanities at me. I couldn't fathom why those children or anyone else could feel so much hatred for someone they didn't even know. Who taught them that? I didn't have to see the pickup truck driver's face to know the answer.

All the hatred percolating in Birmingham boiled over when four young girls inside the 16th Street Baptist Church on September 15, 1963, were killed when it was bombed by the Klan. The church had been an operations center for the mass meetings and marches led by King. Killed were Addie Mae Collins, Carole Robertson, and Cynthia Wesley, all fourteen, and eleven-year-old Denise McNair, who went to my school, Center Street Elementary. Addie Mae's twelve-year-old sister, Sarah, lost an eye in the explosion. She survived but will forever bear the scars, both physical and mental, caused by the explosion.

I met Sarah and her husband, George Rudolph, more than fifty years later in Philadelphia in 2017. I was introduced to them by a mutual friend from Birmingham, Glenn Ellis, who is a health-care ethicist. Sarah is only about an inch or two above five feet, and when she talks about the church bombing in her soft, at times hesitant voice, it's almost like listening to a little girl recall a nightmare she will never forget.

I saw Sarah a second time in 2023 at the National Association of Black Journalists (NABJ) annual convention, which was held in Birmingham. During a panel discussion led by NBC News Today Show cohost Sheinelle Jones, Sarah again recounted the church bombing. "Something like this shouldn't ever happen at a church," she said. "All the glass came rushing in on me, and I was blinded. It was after they operated on my eyes that I found out what happened. As a child I was really angry about what happened to the girls and what had happened to me.

"When I went back to school, they didn't counsel me, and I developed a nervous condition and was so fearful. I was afraid a long time," she said. "When I hear loud sounds and everything, even thunder, it takes me back, and I jump just like a bomb went off. I think about it every day. They had to remove my right eye, and whenever I look into a mirror I just think about, you know, just what happened."

Birmingham had earned the nickname "Bombingham" decades before the church bombing. The Ku Klux Klan in the 1940s began bombing houses occupied by Black families that, in their estimation, were too close to white neighborhoods. But none of those terrorist acts was as heartbreaking as the carnage left by the dynamiting of 16th Street Church.

I didn't know any of the victims, but Denise McNair was a classmate of my brother Jeffery's at Center Elementary School. Her mother, Maxine McNair, taught second grade at Center Street, and her father, Chris McNair, was the White Dairy milkman, whose route included the Loveman Village housing project. I remember seeing him in his white shirt and pants, putting milk bottles on our back porch. McNair had a degree in agronomy from Tuskegee University, but like many Black men and women in the 1960s, he was underemployed.

I got to know Chris in the early 1980s when I wrote several freelance articles for *Down Home*, a Black magazine he founded and ran from the photography studio he opened after Denise's death. Chris was a big man with an engaging personality and ready smile, so it didn't surprise me when he eventually went into politics after the church bombing.

McNair was elected to the state legislature in 1973 and in 1986 became a member of the Jefferson County Commission. Sadly, becoming a commissioner led to his downfall. In 2006, McNair was convicted in federal court of accepting bribes from contractors in exchange for allowing them to work on the county's $3 billion sewer project. "There was no corrupt intent," he told reporters. "But I realize now how it could be perceived. I never thought I did anything wrong."

CHAPTER 5

Appeals delayed McNair's five-year sentence until 2011. That's when I wrote a column as editorial page editor for the *Philadelphia Inquirer*, urging President Obama to pardon the eighty-five-year-old man. I noted that decades had passed before any of three Klansmen who became suspects almost immediately after the church bombing were finally tried and convicted. Two of the by-then elderly Klansmen, Bobby Frank Cherry and Robert "Dynamite Bob" Chambliss, had died in prison by the time McNair was sentenced. I said in my column that it would be a travesty if that same fate befell the father of one of the children murdered by the Klansmen.

"McNair's crime left a bad taste in the mouths of people who were inspired by the story of a man who, in the aftermath of an incredibly heinous, racist act, became a respected leader of blacks and whites. What he did isn't excusable. But it is forgivable," I said.

I asked Obama to pardon McNair "on behalf of a nation that yet owes a debt not just to four little girls killed in a church bombing, but to all civil rights martyrs. Let an old man return to his home. He still has a story to tell, one of remorse, which would be important for the next generation to hear, too." Obama seemed to close his ears to the hundreds of pleas for clemency besides mine. But in 2013, McNair was finally released from prison through a "compassion" program for sick and elderly federal inmates.

Chris's daughter Lisa McNair, who was born a year after her sister died, speculated in her memoir, *Dear Denise*, that the approaching fiftieth anniversary of the 16th Street Church bombing likely led to her father's release. Lisa and her mother attended a White House ceremony where Obama posthumously awarded a Congressional Gold Medal to the four girls slain in the bombing. Chris was suffering from dementia by then, she said, and died six years later, at age ninety-three.

I met Lisa at the same 2023 NABJ convention in Birmingham where Sarah Collins Rudolph spoke during a separate panel discussion of the city's civil rights history. I told her she looked like her father, and with only a hint of a smile, she responded, "I get that a lot." I said I enjoyed her book, which tells her life story in chapters written as letters to the sister she never knew.

Lisa grew up in a much different world than the one that existed when her sister Denise was killed. Lisa went to integrated schools and confesses in her memoir that as an adult she once fell in love with a white man, but he never knew it. She also said she believes her father made some "bad choices," but nothing that amounted to "bribery."

I can't think about Chris without also thinking about Larry Langford, who, like me, grew up in Loveman Village. Larry used to earn pocket change as a child by helping McNair deliver milk. He graduated from the University of Alabama and, after a short stint in the Air Force, became a TV news reporter. We covered some of the same assignments in the mid-1970s, but being on TV made Larry a local celebrity, and he used that fame to be elected mayor of the Fairfield, a neighboring suburb, in 1988.

In 2002 he was elected to the Jefferson County Commission and in 2007 was elected mayor of Birmingham. That's when his star came crashing down. Soon after his mayoral election, Larry was indicted in federal court for allegedly taking bribes when he was a county commissioner to steer bond contracts. He was convicted in 2008 and sentenced to fifteen years. Larry served seven years before being released in 2019 due to his poor health. Suffering from cancer and related issues, Larry died eleven days after his release.

Knowing both Larry and Chris has led me to compare their cases with the cases of two prominent white politicians whom I also knew. Back in the 1970s, several *Birmingham Post-Herald* reporters played touch football with an eclectic group of young professionals that included Al LaPierre, a political lobbyist who in 1982 became executive director of the Alabama Democratic Party, and Don Siegelman, a lawyer who in 1999 was elected governor of Alabama. Both men would later be convicted of corruption but avoided significant prison time.

Siegelman was convicted in 2006 of taking a bribe from the CEO of HealthSouth, a network of rehabilitation hospitals, who in return received an appointment to Alabama's hospital regulatory board. Siegelman was sentenced to seven years in prison, but following several appeals on the grounds that his prosecution was political, the sentence was reduced to ten months. LaPierre was indicted in the same corruption case that snared Langford but, in exchange for his testimony, received a plea deal in which he served less than two years.

I don't think the harsher sentences for Larry and Chris were based on poor legal representation. Neither man was destitute. They should have been able to afford good lawyers. And neither Chris nor Larry had prior criminal records that might have been a factor in their sentencing. Yet, despite each man's poor health while incarcerated, both Chris and Larry spent more time locked up than either Siegelman or LaPierre. All four defendants were convicted of violating the public's trust, but the Black men were sentenced more harshly. Decades after King marched in Alabama for equal treatment, Chris and Larry didn't get it.

CHAPTER 6

SOMETIMES EVIL LEADS TO GOOD

The four girls killed in the 16th Street Baptist Church bombing weren't the only Black children who lost their lives in the racial violence that ensued that day. Johnny Robinson, sixteen, was a shot by a white policeman who said the teenager kept running after being ordered to stop. The officer was never prosecuted. Virgil Ware, thirteen, was shot by a white teenager who claimed Virgil and his brother James had thrown rocks at him while they were riding a bicycle to deliver newspapers. The white boy and a friend were convicted of second-degree manslaughter but served only two years on probation.

Fearing more Klan attacks after the bombing, my father took down the .22 caliber rifle he kept in his bedroom closet and joined other men standing guard in Loveman Village. Every porch light was turned on as they anxiously patrolled the Brickyard in anticipation of what never happened. I was more curious than afraid. The next day my brother Don and I walked to school as if nothing had changed, but were it not for the church bombing, it's unlikely that Congress would have passed either the 1964 Civil Rights Act or the 1965 Voting Rights Act.

Without the bombing, it's unlikely that racial attitudes in Birmingham would have softened as much as they did, allowing previously shut doors to open for Black children. One such door opened in 1968 and led to my becoming the first Black member of the Birmingham Youth Presbytery. The race of its congregation and its small size, with fewer than two hundred members, made Westminster an odd choice to have a Youth Presbytery member. But our church's very existence was also odd. Westminster was part of the Presbyterian Church of the United States, which was formed by churches in the Southern states that seceded from the Union during the Civil War. Birmingham's only other Black Presbyterian church, Miller Memorial, was part of the Presbyterian Church of the USA, which stood with the North during war.

The Birmingham Youth Presbytery met at various city and suburban churches but never at Westminster during my tenure. We mostly would discuss what we, as teenagers, could do to help spread the Gospel. We also attended youth convocations usually held on weekends or during the summer at Presbyterian youth camps in Alabama, Tennessee, and Florida. There was never more than a handful of Black participants, if that many.

I never said it, but at times, in my head, I questioned whether the youth group really had a purpose. Like during a Bible study retreat in Ocala, Florida, when we fasted for a day to make us more sensitive to the plight of America's hungry families but later gorged ourselves with multiple bowls of ice cream at a nearby Howard Johnson's. Suspecting I may have been alone in my feelings, I never expressed them to anyone else.

My roommate during a different weekend retreat at Camp NaCoMe in Pleasantville, Tennessee, was Tom Hay, the affable son of the pastor of a suburban church in Homewood. One morning as I combed my hair, Tom politely apologized before asking why I even bothered. I laughed before explaining that a Black man's hair didn't need to fall across his eyes to need grooming. But I didn't mind Tom asking. It felt good to know my presence among white kids might help dispel some of the stereotypes and myths they associated with Black people.

Later that weekend an adult counselor asked if he could borrow my knife to cut one of the watermelons being served as an afternoon snack to campers. Without thinking I blurted, "Not all Black people carry knives!" After a few seconds of silence, everyone grinned nervously and I almost forgot about it. But that evening, during the camp-wide meeting we held each evening, at least a dozen people softly muttered "racism" when congregants were asked to stand and confess a sin.

Their repenting made me wonder how many of my fellow campers lacked the courage to publicly admit the same transgression. But then, given my own prejudice that was justifiably based, I believed, on how Black folks continued to be mistreated long after slavery and segregation, maybe I should have also stood up and confessed.

CHAPTER 7

DADDY'S STROKE CHANGED EVERYTHING

One night in July 1967, while moonlighting as a janitor for an office building in Birmingham's Black business district, Daddy had a stroke that left him unable to speak and needing help to walk. I was fourteen years old and could see in Daddy's eyes how hard it was for him to accept being disabled. He and Mama both hated asking anyone for help, a trait they passed down to their sons.

Mama tried to take care of Daddy after he was released from Spain Rehabilitation Hospital but put him in a nursing home after school began and she no longer had help tending to Daddy's bathroom and other needs in our two-level apartment. Daddy was in the nursing home only about a month before he died on September 13, 1967.

The coroner attributed Daddy's death to another stroke. I think Daddy wanted to die. He could no longer speak, no longer walk, and his mournful gaze when he was still home with us suggested to me that he had lost his will to live. I want to believe Daddy found comfort in death, but that was not the case for Mama. She seemed overwhelmed with remorse for having put Daddy in a nursing home.

"I did the best I can," she moaned over and over again at Daddy's funeral, which was held two blocks from our church at Smith & Gaston Funeral Home. Mama said that was only right, given Daddy's mostly ignoring Westminster. The service was short, the gathering small. Daddy was then buried a few miles away at Grace Hill Cemetery.

DADDY'S STROKE CHANGED EVERYTHING

Leaving the funeral, Miss Goldie, an office worker for R. B. Broyes Furniture Co., where Daddy worked, walked over to me and my brothers. "Your daddy was a powerful man," she said, and walked away.

Over the years I have thought about her comment but still don't know for certain what she meant. Perhaps she was referring to nothing more than Daddy's ability to lift heavy furniture every day on the job. Or maybe she was referring to how hard Daddy worked to provide for his family of seven. His perseverance certainly required great strength.

I wish Daddy had lived long enough to regain his ability to speak. Maybe then he could have told me how his "power," even after death, impressed people like Miss Goldie.

Born July 14, 1909, Lewis Jackson, my father, was the son of Rebecca and Jefferson Jackson in Brewton, a small town in Escambia County, Alabama. Lewis's grandparents were Margaret and Berry Jackson. Berry was a farmer in Repton, thirty miles north of Brewton in Conecuh County. Born in 1824, Berry most likely had been a slave. Only about 2 percent of Black people living in Alabama before the Civil War were free. Half of those free Black people lived in Mobile, but that was ninety miles from Brewton, and laws restricting their movement prevented much traveling between the two towns.

If he was a slave, Berry most likely was owned by someone named Jackson. Slaves freed after the war often assumed the surnames of their former masters. There were 4,367 slaves in Conecuh County in 1850, according to the US Census, and three slaveholders in the county named Jackson: A. E. Jackson, who had fourteen slaves; D. Jackson, ten slaves; and W. S. Jackson, nine slaves. Berry Jackson's name first appears in the 1870 census, the nation's first after the Civil War. He and his wife, Margaret, were counted as a married couple and his occupation was listed as farm laborer, but that was changed to blacksmith in the 1880 census, which also stated that Berry tilled twenty acres of rented land. He was a tenant farmer.

Berry and Margaret may have married as slaves before the Civil War. Some slaveowners permitted that, and the Jackson's four daughters and three sons were born between 1859 and 1876. Jefferson Jackson, born in 1874, was their third son and my father's father. In 1904, Jefferson married my grandmother, Rebecca Brooks, whom I only vaguely remember as "Mama Jack."

Family legend is that she was of Native American descent, but there is no record of that. My older brothers say her hair was usually braided in long plaits, which might imply Native American heritage, but that's no proof. My clearest

CHAPTER 7

memory of Mama Jack is seeing her in her coffin during her funeral in Brewton in 1961. I was seven years old.

Jeff and Rebecca had three daughters and three sons. Their middle son, Lewis, was my father. Daddy left Brewton for Birmingham when he was about eighteen. I found his name and address in a 1928 city directory that showed him living in a boarding house. His listed occupation was "shoe polisher."

Daddy later found a better-paying job in the coal mines surrounding Birmingham and moved into a Shelby County boarding house close to where he worked. But by the early 1930s, he left the life-sapping coal mines and became a chauffeur for Harold M. Henderson, a wealthy real estate appraiser and president of Birmingham's first zoning board, a combination that seems like a conflict of interests. Henderson's daughter, Martha Henderson Goings, was an artist during the so-called Ashcan art movement of that era in New York, and was known for her paintings depicting African American neighborhoods.

Now working in the city, Daddy rented a room in the mostly Black Titusville section of southwest Birmingham. His landlords were steel mill worker Luther Bell and his wife, Esther, whom friends called "Bama." A second boarder in the Bells' home was a man named Isaac, whom Daddy called "Zook" when we met him years later as children.

The Bells' house was less than a mile from our housing project apartment in Loveman Village, and our family infrequently visited them to watch their television. I remember one evening when we were watching the 1960s sci-fi thriller *The Outer Limits*, and it began with its warning that viewers should not attempt to change channels because extraterrestrial forces had temporarily taken control of their TV. Trying to get better reception, Uncle Bell, which is what we called him, started trying to adjust the TV's antenna, only to have a seemingly terrified Aunt Esther shout, "Bell, they told you they control the TV!" We brothers stifled our laughter, not wanting to embarrass such a sweet person.

The Bells lived only two or three blocks from where Mama lived for several years before she married. That was when Mama was living with her aunt Hannah, and her husband, Lee Thomas. Mama may have first met Daddy when he was a boarder in the Bells' home, but I'm not certain, because as good of a news reporter as I claim to be, I never asked. When I was a child, it never entered my mind that Mama and Daddy weren't always married. But even after, in her old age, she moved in with my wife, Denice, and me, I never thought to ask.

What I do know, because I have their marriage certificate as proof, is that Mama and Daddy were married on June 16, 1945. My brother Anthony was born fifteen months later in 1946; Jeffery, in 1950; Don, in 1952; and I, eighteen months later, in 1953. Mama told me that a St. Vincent's Hospital nurse had suggested that I be named after one of Birmingham's most popular country-Western radio disc jockeys, "Happy Hal" Burns. Guess I was a happy baby. Calvin, the last brother born, arrived in 1957.

Daddy's job delivering furniture didn't provide enough money to feed and clothe a family of seven, so he also worked nights as a janitor in the Pythian Temple, an office building in Birmingham's Black business district. Daddy's two-note whistle signaling his arrival home from his day job always sent us boys scampering to the back door to greet him. Mama always had dinner ready to greet him. He then had a few hours to rest before taking the bus to his night job.

When he wasn't working, Daddy was likely sitting in our living room, smoking a cigar, maybe having a beer, watching a ball game or boxing match on TV, or dozing in his chair.

We didn't have a car, so the truck Daddy drove to deliver furniture for R. B. Broyles occasionally served as our family vehicle. I was thrilled whenever Daddy surprised us by showing up at our elementary school in the big green truck to take us home, friends included. We would use the quilts that were in the truck to protect furniture and pretend we were hiding in caves. Sometimes between deliveries Daddy parked his truck outside our apartment building, and we would climb into its roomy cab and pretend we were driving somewhere nowhere near Loveman Village. I knew there had to be better places to live, but as a child I didn't know how to get there.

CHAPTER 8

FINDING STRENGTH IN OUR CHURCH

Mama didn't remarry after Daddy died. She told us she didn't want another man trying to discipline us, which seemed a stretch given our ages. Three of us were teenagers, and Skippy was twenty-one. Even so, I didn't mind her decision. No one could replace Daddy. But someone came close. A strong bond eventually developed between Mama and a longtime family friend, Henry LeVert, who coincidentally also delivered furniture, but for Loveman's department store, not R. B. Broyles.

That's where the similarity ended. Henry was a regular church goer who liked to tell jokes. Daddy rarely did either of those two things. Henry and Mama liked to watch TV together and occasionally went out to eat. He was a good man and always treated Mama with respect, but I couldn't envision anyone taking Daddy's place. Henry died about ten years before Mama, who lived to be ninety-three. His death made me realize how wrong I had been in dismissing him as a suitable husband for Mama.

Sometimes it takes a death to open our eyes to what was always staring us in the face. Before Daddy died, I never thought of my family's poverty as the lens through which some people would see and judge us, interact with us. Which is why I was troubled somewhat when church members brought us a Thanksgiving basket about two months after his death.

I couldn't help thinking we had never been treated like a charity case before Daddy's death, but maybe that's how some of the church's more affluent members had always seen us. Maybe that's what the teachers, lawyers, and other professionals who attended Westminster thought of its only family from the projects. I didn't resent receiving a Thanksgiving basket, but it did make me think more about our family's shakier financial situation now that Daddy was gone.

We were living off Daddy's Social Security benefits and whatever my oldest brother, Anthony, kicked in from the jobs he held while also attending college. But when bills started to back up, Mama, at age fifty-one, returned to a routine she had quit thirty years earlier, joining dozens of other Black women on the buses that took them over Red Mountain to clean and cook in the suburban homes of white families. Occasionally, Mama would also bring laundry home to wash and iron for extra money. What she refused to do was apply for welfare or food stamps. Mama said the government asked too many questions to give you a little bit of money.

That was her pride talking. That same pride made sure her boys always wore freshly laundered shirts and creased jeans to school. If patches were needed, Mama always placed them inside our pants or shirts and sewed them so any visible stitches might seem more decorative than necessary. She had been just as meticulous about Daddy's clothes, always sending him to work in starched, creased uniforms that looked as if they had been professionally laundered.

Mama's pride was always on full display when she visited our elementary school for the individual parent-teacher meetings held once a year at Alabama's public schools during American Education Week. Mama was always fashionable but never flashy when she dressed up, and her demure hairstyles and modest makeup typically matched her conservative attire. She would listen intently to everything our teachers said about her sons' academic progress and conduct, never raising her voice if she felt a response was needed.

Mama wanted our teachers to see her children's good manners weren't by accident. We didn't need daily reminders from Mama on how to behave. We knew full well what our fates would be if we ever came home from school with a bad conduct grade. It was similarly drilled into us to never to ask anyone for anything. We didn't want anyone at any time to think the Jackson family might need charity.

Mama got angry enough to spit venom one day when I told her I had accepted a dime from a classmate, Clarence Fortune, to ride the bus home during a rainstorm. Just the look on her face screamed at me "never again!"

CHAPTER 8

Any suggestion of poverty hurt Mama's pride. But she relished opportunities to show her sons that money wasn't the best way gauge a person's worth.

Mama couldn't have been prouder than the day she hosted our church's women's Bible study group, which was called the Ladies Circle. Whatever fears the ladies had prior to arriving for tea in the projects were calmed by Mama's hospitality, immaculate apartment, delectable finger sandwiches, and, of course, coconut cake.

Three of those women—Mattie Brown, Evelyn Glover, and Annye Downing—remained faithful friends to Mama over the years even after she left Alabama to live with my family first in Maryland and later New Jersey. They called and wrote letters to stay connected. After Mama died in 2009, Mrs. Glover and Mrs. Downing would occasionally write or call me. Mrs. Brown had died, too, by then. The ladies would ask me about my family and my brothers and voice their concern about Westminster's future.

Like many mainline Protestant churches, Black and white, Westminster's attendance had declined to levels that threatened its continued existence. Our conversations typically ended with the ladies telling me what a fine woman Mama was. I appreciated that even after Mama's death, they felt it important for me to know the Jacksons were still part of the Westminster family.

CHAPTER 9

HIGH SCHOOL CAN BE SCARY

My oldest brother, Anthony, graduated from Ullman High School three years before I became a freshman there in 1967, but Jeffery and Don were still there to show me the ropes. Their reputation as good students who stayed out of trouble was helpful in my classes with teachers who knew them. But Ullman itself took some getting used to after eight years in an elementary school where younger students seemed largely innocent. Some Ullman kids showed up for first period roll call either drunk, hung over, or high. Even so, boys' adviser Thomas Hill managed most situations, with gym teachers James Pettus, Sylvester Campbell, and Heywood Gibson available if their muscles were needed.

Walking to and from Ullman took me through some tough neighborhoods, but although Loveman Village also had a reputation for violence, my brothers and I considered it safe ground. We had lived in the projects most of our young lives and had known some gang members since we were children. Our mutual respect seemed to grow over the years as we Jacksons avoided the pitfalls that had already sent some of them to a juvenile detention facility, if not prison.

That respect seemed to grow after my big brother Anthony got out of the Air Force and bought a car. More than a few times he was asked to take someone we knew to the hospital after they had been stabbed or shot. Fortunately, none of them died. Less-powerful handguns back then weren't as lethal as today's higher-caliber weapons.

I never knew when an encounter with some wannabe tough guy outside

CHAPTER 9

the friendly confines of Loveman Village might take a turn for the worse. Ullman also had students from the Southtown housing project, which was closer to it than Loveman Village, as well as students from a lower-income neighborhood of single-family homes near Memorial Park and across the street from the Birmingham Jail. But it wasn't just neighborhood gangs I had to fear; there were also those large families of brothers, sisters, cousins, and other relatives that might as well have been gangs. Fights with one relative could easily become fights with them all.

During my freshman and sophomore years at Ullman, I mostly walked to and from school with my brother Don before he graduated in 1969. Don's typical response to belligerence is to stare it in the eye. Back then, thugs seeking cash would shake down students walking home by demanding they pay a toll to pass them. One day, Don and I encountered two such bandits brandishing knives as they blocked a walkway underneath the Sixth Avenue overpass. They demanded money, not knowing that Don was not only the most stubborn of us Jackson brothers, even Calvin, but likely the most stubborn person they would ever meet.

Don wasn't about to pay tribute to two teenagers who didn't appear mentally prepared to do battle. Without a hint of hesitation, he told them as much, and after some agitated jawing back and forth that revealed the would-be highwaymen weren't all that eager to back up their threats, they stepped aside. Don is six-foot-three, so maybe they were intimidated by his superior size. What's more likely, I think, is that the look in Don's eyes told them he would put up a bigger fight than they wanted. Either way, they let us pass.

A similar experience after Don had left Ullman for college showed just how different two brothers can be. My friend Charles and I were walking home when we were approached by two scruffy teenagers in Memorial Park. They were demanding money from anyone who didn't want to take a longer detour around the park, and because I'm not Don, I resorted to my usual response to intimidation, which is to try to talk my way out of a fight. But, perhaps in haste, I didn't carefully choose my words.

"Man, do you think we would be walking instead of riding the bus if we had any money?" I said. "Say what!" screamed one guy as he approached me menacingly with his pocketknife drawn. But the other kid, maybe accepting the logic of my claim or maybe disliking what would have been the likely sight of blood if I were stabbed, laid a restraining hand on his partner, and after briefly exchanging glances, they let us pass.

Charles and I didn't say another word but burst out laughing once we exited the park. We were teenagers, which made it easy to disregard the potential for disaster in that brief moment and enjoy the exhilaration of somehow finding a way to avoid a crueler fate.

Knowing Charles since first grade means we share many memories. Like the time Ullman's choir director, Gregory Durr White, who sometimes drove us home after practice, left us in her double-parked car while she tried to run a quick errand inside a downtown building. Sure enough, it wasn't long before cars stuck behind us began to blow their horns. We had taken driver's ed, but neither Charles nor I was licensed. Nevertheless, he got behind the wheel, determined to move the vehicle, but he couldn't properly parallel park it.

We were sure the police would be called, but just in time we saw a man we knew from Loveman Village whom we asked to properly park the car for us. Mrs. White never questioned how her car got parked, and we thought it best not to tell her we weren't able to park it. Maybe she was watching the whole time and wanted to see how we would handle the situation. But that would mean risking damage to her car, so that's unlikely. Either way, we learned another important lesson: never hesitate to ask for help when the situation demands it.

Mrs. White, one of Birmingham's most venerated Black educators, was also choir director at Sixth Avenue Baptist Church. For decades, her dedication had provided a sturdy platform upon which Ullman students could excel beyond their musical studies. I never knew why she took a liking to two alley cats from the projects like Charles and me. At least Charles had a magnificent baritone voice, while I could barely hold a tune. Maybe she felt my tagging along for the ride would help maintain Charles's interest in the choir. More likely, I hope, she saw potential in both of us, and her friendship alone encouraged us, even in situations when she never spoke a word.

During segregation, Black teachers like Mrs. White were why their students could achieve goals supposedly unattainable for children who were deprived of the better books, materials, and facilities provided to white children. I'm not sure what I would have become in life had it not been for teachers like Mrs. White who took advantage of opportunities outside the classroom to teach us how to take responsibility for our lives instead of allowing someone else to dictate our course. Sometimes those teachers seemed to purposely put us in in stressful situations so we could figure out how to overcome adversity in unfamiliar settings.

CHAPTER 10

INTRODUCTION TO JOURNALISM

I didn't think of journalism as a possible career until I was in high school. Sure, I read newspapers and watched TV news, but I had no real understanding of how reporters and editors did their jobs. That changed after my ninth grade English teacher, Reva Coleman, took notice of my aptitude for writing and suggested I write for the *Wolf Call*, Ullman's student newspaper. I wrote articles about campus events that were then edited by the paper's student adviser, Kathryn Robinson.

I thought I was doing well but was surprised when she and Mrs. Coleman recommended me to be a participant in the University of Alabama's annual journalism workshop for high school students. Thanks to them, just five years after George Wallace "stood in the schoolhouse door" to keep Alabama segregated, I became a student at the university.

Of course, Wallace only stood in the door of Foster Auditorium long enough to seemingly fulfill a campaign promise to block integration of any public school. He stepped away after President John F. Kennedy federalized the Alabama National Guard and ordered it to assist in the governor's physical removal, if necessary.

Kennedy's intervention allowed Vivian Malone Jones and James Hood to be registered at Alabama, but they weren't the first Black students to do that. Autherine Lucy Foster enrolled at the university in 1956, two years year after the US Supreme Court's historic *Brown v. Board* ruling, but university officials expelled her three days later, purportedly for her own protection due to the racial violence that was rocking the campus.

An interview I did with Ms. Foster two decades later earned me a $100 bonus from United Press International. My interview in 1982 won UPI's monthly Southern Horizons award for best feature story. By then, Alabama had one thousand nine hundred Black students, including Ms. Foster's daughter. She told me those Black students and the ones yet to come were why she went through the "hell" of trying to break segregation's back at the university. "They don't have to go through what I went through, and that's what it was all about," she said.

I didn't know anything about Ms. Foster when I arrived at Alabama for the high school journalism workshop in 1968, but I knew I was in unfamiliar territory—not only because of my race, but because at age fourteen, I had never spent a night away from home. The empty liquor bottles left on a shelf in my Paty Hall dorm room provided a hint of student life at Alabama. But it being summer, the campus was mostly empty. I missed my own bed but felt safe enough amid the relative silence of my dormitory room to fall asleep.

I was the only Black student in the two-week journalism workshop, and there weren't many Black college students on campus that summer either. I met a few one day who were outside the dining hall where I ate meals. I told them I was from Birmingham, and one girl said she was from Eutaw. Not being familiar with the small town south of Tuscaloosa, I asked her which city in Utah. The college students all laughed before me filling me in on the local geography.

I would see the same students occasionally on campus and wave, but that was the extent of our connection. I concluded they thought they were too mature to hang out with a fourteen-year-old. But it could be they thought I was hanging out with the other workshop participants. If so, they were wrong. The white kids weren't mean to me, just distant. I don't recall having a single conversation with any of them outside of our classroom. Maybe that's why I don't remember any of their names.

If the white students got together after our daily workshop sessions, they never invited me to join them. That didn't bother me too much. Having spent very little time with white people, I didn't relish feeling on edge in anticipation of becoming the object of some racist slight or trying to ignore an insult uttered to put me in my place. Each afternoon after our workshop classes ended, I would take long walks around campus before heading back for dinner, and then I would watch TV in the dorm's lounge until it was time for bed.

CHAPTER 10

The only time the white students in the workshop invited me to join them was when one boy asked if I needed a ride to the restaurant off campus where a dinner marking the workshop's two-week conclusion was being held. Five of us fit into the boy's small car. We chatted about the workshop and our high schools. The conversation seemed to come so easily that I wished we had gotten to know each other better during our time on campus. The next day, my brother Anthony drove me home from Tuscaloosa, and I wondered what the white kids would tell their parents about probably the first Black person they ever knew.

Not making new friends didn't diminish my experience at the university. Associate professor Miriam G. Hill ran the workshop and never said or did anything that suggested I was incapable of doing the same work as the white students. We interviewed and wrote stories about people both on campus and in Tuscaloosa. We wrote the headlines for our work, and while we didn't take photographs, we did discuss how each article might be illustrated.

Professor Hill's fairness in assessing our work gave me confidence in my abilities. Bolstered by her encouragement, I started believing I could become a journalist. Writing stories about people in the university community helped me see how people living seemingly disparate lives are connected in ways they don't even think about.

I realized journalists can tell stories that help people connect the dots. Journalists can tell stories that help Black and white people acknowledge their common bonds. Journalists can even help dispel the types of stereotypes that just might have been why the white kids in our workshop rarely said more than "hello" to the Black boy in their class. I wanted to be a journalist.

CHAPTER 11

"WE DON'T WANT TO INTEGRATE"

The high school journalism workshop at the University of Alabama was my first time being educated side by side with white students, but not my last. My second experience was neither voluntary nor desired. At least, not initially.

A court-ordered desegregation plan in 1970 closed Ullman High School just months before my senior year was to begin. Birmingham's new attendance zones sent me and hundreds of other Ullman students to Ramsay High, which, as a result, went from being 95 percent white to being 50 percent Black. The court order also sent hundreds of Ullman students, including my best friend since first grade, Charles Abron, to Parker High School.

Founded in 1900, Parker was Birmingham's first Black high school. Ullman was founded in 1937 and immediately became Parker's archrival in sports and scholastics. Three more Black high schools were opened later, including Western Olin, 1952; Carver, 1959; and Hayes, 1960. They competed athletically as the Big Five until integration ended the all-Black league. Just like that, traditional rivalries that had lasted generations were tossed aside.

The desegregation plan's seemingly arbitrary attendance lines split Loveman Village in half, sending Charles and me our separate ways. Consequently, all the groundwork we had laid to prepare for our senior year at Ullman was for nothing. Before that, the only setback to my plans for the twelfth grade was losing the election to become the next school year's student council president.

CHAPTER 11

My brother Jeffery was student council president when he was a senior, but he had what I sorely lacked—charisma.

I lost to James Payne, who not only was on the basketball team but wore GQ quality outfits to school that he purchased for discount prices from the men's store where he worked part time. Maybe losing the election was for the best, since I wouldn't have gotten to serve anyway.

I didn't want to go to Ramsay, but once there I couldn't help but be impressed by how much better equipped its classrooms were and how much better prepared, but not smarter, many of my new classmates were. My most important lesson, however, had nothing to do with books or the classroom. I learned not all white children were like Wally and Beaver or the other sit-com kids I watched on TV.

I learned that some white teens, just like some Black teens, were in gangs, some smoked cigarettes, some liked to drink beer and wine, some smoked weed or took other drugs, and some got pregnant. Maybe that's why their parents wanted to keep us segregated, I thought, so that we wouldn't recognize that, skin color aside, Black teenagers and white teenagers are more alike than they are different.

I don't recall even one fight involving race at Ramsay while I was there. The only incident that came even remotely close to that was when a gym teacher paired me and a white boy about my size to wrestle. After some pushing and shoving that, after an interminable length of time, took us down to the gym floor, we rolled around like two pigs in a trough competing for slop, neither getting an advantage over the other, until the coach got tired of watching us sweat and told us to quit.

It took me a while to catch up academically, but when it was time to graduate, the 1971 class chose Gail Horne and me as the seniors most likely to succeed. Gail, who was also senior class president, became an attorney after college and was later elected a district judge in Louisiana. We had known each other since we both attended all-Black Center Street Elementary School, but Gail and a few other Center Street students started Ramsay as freshmen. That distinction became more meaningful to me at our fiftieth reunion.

COVID was still a plague in 2021, so the reunion was virtual. Even so, only about thirty of Ramsay's 1971 graduates participated in the Zoom gathering. Most of them were Black and still lived in Birmingham. I signed in from Texas, where I settled after retiring from the *Houston Chronicle*. Each of us was allowed to say a few words about our days at Ramsay. While I mostly said good things, I also mentioned how "traumatic" it had been to be reassigned to a different school after spending three years anticipating a glorious senior year at Ullman.

I didn't think I had said anything wrong, but Shandra Jackson, who, like Gail and me, had also attended Center Street Elementary School, said she didn't see anything "traumatic" about what I experienced. She didn't explain why she felt that way, and surprised by her reaction, I didn't ask. Later, I thought about what Shandra said, and I think I understand why she said it.

Shandra, Gail, and others in that very small group of Black students who integrated Ramsay in the 1960s undoubtedly experienced much worse than what the seeming multitude of Ullman expatriates who arrived in 1970 experienced. In a setting other than a Zoom reunion, we might have talked about that and I might have asked Shandra if, after enduring all she did to integrate Ramsay, it would have been "traumatic" to be involuntarily transferred to another school right before her senior year began.

Over the years, I have concluded that while forced integration wasn't easy for its involuntary participants, it was necessary at the time, and considering the lessons I learned both inside and outside my classrooms at Ramsay, I'm glad I was a participant.

My grades at Ramsay and college entrance exam scores won me a four-year journalism scholarship in 1971 from the Coca-Cola USA foundation and the National Newspaper Publishers Association (NNPA), a Black organization. I was flown to Atlanta to receive the award a few weeks before my graduation. It was my first time on an airplane and first time staying in a hotel. The lavish Regency Hyatt House had a glass elevator in its atrium, which allowed you to see Atlanta's skyline. I can't tell you how many times I rode that elevator just for the view.

The scholarship was presented to me during a dinner by a marketing executive for Coca-Cola, Harold Hamilton, and Emory O. Jackson, editor of the *Birmingham World*, one of Birmingham's two weekly Black newspapers, the other being the *Birmingham Times*. I was so caught up in the moment I didn't notice that the first and last names of the men who presented my award were Harold and Jackson.

I felt honored to meet Emory O. Jackson, who I believe should be considered just as much a champion for civil rights in Birmingham as the Reverends Fred Shuttlesworth and Martin Luther King Jr., even though he disagreed with their confrontation tactics. As the first president of the Alabama

CHAPTER 11

NAACP, Jackson crisscrossed the state to make speeches in churches, on college campuses, and other forums to promote integration.

But like many among Birmingham's Black establishment who didn't want King to come to town, Jackson believed more could be accomplished by registering Black voters and changing America through legislation and the courts than by marching. After the 16th Street Baptist Church bombing in 1963, Jackson said Black people should "pour into the churches on Sunday, stream to the voter-registration offices, make their dollars talk freedom, and build up a better leadership." He wasn't wrong, but marching and boycotting were necessary too.

The Coca-Cola/NNPA scholarship required me to attend a college or university with an accredited journalism program, which ironically, in 1971, left out most of the historically Black institutions. That didn't matter much, however, because I had already decided to take a different path: far from Birmingham and completely unlike the segregated Black schools where I was educated all years but my senior.

I chose Baker University, a small college in tiny, almost all-white Baldwin City, Kansas. My only connection to Baker was that it was only about twenty-five miles from Olathe, Kansas, where my brother Anthony was once stationed when he was in the Air Force.

Only fifty of Baker's eight hundred students were Black when I arrived, but it was actually very diverse. I met students from Botswana, Kenya, Nigeria, Rhodesia, Malaysia, India, China, Hong Kong, Korea, the Philippines, Iran, Lebanon, Venezuela, England, Germany, and Norway. Most of its American students were from Kansas or Missouri, but at least twenty other states were represented, and more than a dozen students were Indigenous Americans, several of whom had attended nearby Haskell Indian Junior College in Lawrence.

I thought Baker would be a good place for a Black kid from Birmingham's housing projects to get a hugely different perspective on life. I also thought going to a small college would complement the individualized instruction I had received as the first Black participant in the University of Alabama's summer workshop for high school journalism students. And I thought the three summers of dorm life I had experienced as a participant in the Upward Bound program at historically Black Miles College in Fairfield had prepared me to leave home and make it on my own.

Both my friend Charles and I had participated in Upward Bound, a federally funded program for underprivileged high school students. We were tutored by Miles professors in English, math, science, and Black history every

Saturday during the school year, and we lived in dormitory rooms on campus for about six weeks each summer. Best of all, Upward Bound participants also received a weekly ten-dollar stipend, which I typically spent buying stylishly mod clothes at the New Ideal department store or the latest 45s at a popular record shop.

Upward Bound students received individual counseling to help us successfully apply for college. To help us choose a preferred college, we routinely took weekend bus trips to historically Black colleges and universities (HBCUs) in the South, including Tuskegee, Stillman, Alabama A&M, and Alabama State in our home state, as well as Fisk in Tennessee; Morehouse, Spelman, and Clark in Georgia; Howard in Washington, DC; Tougaloo and Jackson State in Mississippi; and Bethune-Cookman in Florida.

Living on an HBCU campus every summer for three years as an Upward Bound participant in a way prepared me to become a Black student at historically white Baker University. Miles students and professors who participated in the civil rights movement believed it was their duty to raise the consciousness of their high school mentees.

They wanted us to know what was at stake in the battles being waged not only by the NAACP, Southern Christian Leadership Conference, and Student Nonviolent Coordinating Committee, but also by the Black Panthers. They recommended books we should read and introduced us to spoken word revolutionaries such as Gil Scott-Heron, Nikki Giovanni, bell hooks, and the Last Poets. They taught us to love ourselves as young, gifted, and Black students being educated to give back to our people.

Filled with knowledge imparted by my Miles mentors, I was eager to join Baker's Black student union (BSU) as a freshman and became its president my junior year. Our BSU was called Mungano, a derivative of the Swahili word for union or alliance. Each campus organization was required to have a faculty adviser, but there were no full-time Black faculty members on campus during my freshman year. Instead, Mungano's adviser was the Reverend Hugh Stouppe, a sixty-six-year-old white English professor who also had been a Christian missionary in China.

I still smile at a 1972 yearbook photo of Mungano members, including silver-haired, cardigan-clad, bespectacled Professor Stouppe, each one of us standing with a raised fist symbolizing Black power.

Most of Baker's white students considered Mungano a Black fraternity or sorority because it had a student government seat, fielded intramural sports

CHAPTER 11

teams, and organized parties and other events on campus, but our goals were more than social. Mungano protests following a fight on campus between Black and white students forced Baker's president to cancel all classes for a day of introspection to discuss race relations in small groups.

We routinely brought civil rights activists from Kansas City and even other states to campus, including the Reverend Cecil L. Murray of San Francisco, a leader of the liberation theology movement, and humorist Dick Gregory, who marched with the Reverend Martin Luther King Jr. in Birmingham.

After his lecture on campus, Gregory chatted with Mungano members in the apartment I shared with two friends. The vegetarian and fasting proponent also believed in seeing auras. Sitting in our living room, he drew a picture of the energy field that he said he saw surrounding my persona. But I couldn't find the drawing after he left, so maybe he got my karma wrong.

My roommates were Ricky Fisher, who was from Washington, DC, and Clarence "Bud" Mays, from Kansas City. Bud had two cousins who were also students at Baker: sisters Brenda and Denice Pledger. Denice and I eventually became a couple. So did Brenda and Ricky. None of us knew when we met as freshmen that we were meeting our future spouses.

I often complained about Baker being small when I was a student, but I actually liked the campus. It was bigger than Miles but had enough sidewalks that you never needed a car to get to any point on campus. Founded in 1858 by Methodists, Baker is Kansas's oldest four-year college. Still funded by the United Methodist Church when I arrived in 1971, the school required all students to attend convocations at Baldwin United Methodist Church until my sophomore year.

But Baker was far from being a strictly religious institution. You could tell that by the number of weekend keg parties. Baker had nine fraternities and sororities, but while I was there, only about eight Black men and maybe two Black women became members of the white Greek organizations. Greeks dominated Baker's social scene, but house parties thrown by off-campus students were also part of the mix. Black students might show up anywhere, but we mostly partied by ourselves wherever we could, off or on campus.

Less than a decade after segregation was no longer legal anywhere in America, some of us were still getting used to socializing with white people, still processing the world as the dual citizens DuBois described, finding comfort whenever we could fully be ourselves without worrying about what white folks might think.

Baker was only fifteen miles from Lawrence, home to the University of Kansas, which provided another outlet for social life, including bars and restaurants, if you could get there, meaning if you had a car. Only two or three Black students had a car during my entire four years at Baker. The rest of us piled in whenever we got a chance, mostly to head to a package store nine miles away in Edgerton, where you could buy hard liquor, wine, and real beer. Kansas law required taverns like the two in Baldwin to only sell beer with less than a 3.2 percent alcohol content.

But I didn't choose Baker in search of an active social life. The small college environment I sought was all that I had hoped for. Having sixty faculty members for eight hundred students provided the level of personal interaction with instructors that I wanted. My roommate Clarence Mays and I were the only two students in a senior political science class taught by Karen Horvath. When the weather was right, the three of us would sit under a tree and discuss geopolitical theory.

Baker's coziness allowed my journalism professors, Beverly Paulson and Richard Lindeborg, to pay close attention to their students' strengths and weaknesses and better guide those who might find a career in journalism. We learned mostly the basics by putting out a weekly student newspaper, so I wasn't sure when my graduation approached if I knew enough to get a job. I really didn't know what I wanted to do after graduation.

Il Roh Suh, one of my political science professors when I was a senior, advised me to take the State Department's foreign service officer test. I was tempted but instead applied to the graduate journalism schools at Syracuse University and the University of Georgia. I was accepted by both schools but in the end decided I didn't want to take on more student debt.

The thought of going back to Birmingham to look for a job was scary too. The only jobs I'd ever had were work-study positions at Baker and summer gigs when school was out. None of them had anything to do with journalism, but each experience taught me lessons about people, life, and myself that in their own ways were priceless. I thought about each of those experiences while making up my mind about my next move.

CHAPTER 12

COULDN'T SHAKE GEORGE WALLACE'S HAND

I took out student loans and had work-study jobs to pay for what my scholarships didn't cover at Baker University. First I was a residence hall assistant at Horn Hall and later a technician handling microphones, lighting, and other equipment at Rice Auditorium. My boss at the auditorium was J. Ward "Sparky" Spielman, a tiny man whose routinely deadpan face belied his good humor. Sparky occasionally let me earn extra cash running the projector at Baldwin City's only movie theater, the Gem, which had maybe one hundred seats. Sparky owned the Gem.

I never had a job before going to college. That might be a rite of passage for some teenagers, but Mama and Daddy worried that if their sons earned extra money working part time after school, we might not pursue a college education. Of course, Mama gave us plenty of work at home. She taught us to cook, clean house, even sew a little, explaining that we shouldn't depend on a woman to do anything we could do for ourselves.

That directive seemed a corollary to Mama's other warning to not "go round sniffing after some piss-tail girl." I didn't realize that commandment wasn't sacrosanct until I was in sixth grade and developed my first crush on a girl. Mama may have raised an eyebrow when I told her I wanted to give Robbie Mathis a Christmas present, but instead of launching into a sermon on the wiles of wicked women, she bought me a nice comb-and-brush set to give Robbie. Daddy stayed out of the conversation.

My working during summer breaks was no problem for Mama once I got into college. Daddy had died, and she struggled to make sure her sons in college returned to their campuses each fall with proper clothing and some pocket cash. Mama appreciated whatever we could do for ourselves financially, but an additional benefit for me was learning lessons far removed from academia that would never leave me.

Following my freshman year at Baker, I applied for work through Birmingham's summer jobs program for youths and was hired as an aide in Spain Rehabilitation Hospital's audiology department. I was at Spain when Governor George Wallace arrived for rehab after being shot while campaigning for president in a Laurel, Maryland, shopping center. Wallace was paralyzed when one of the four bullets fired by Arthur Bremer lodged in his spine. Bremer, an apparently delusional man who said he also wanted to shoot President Richard Nixon, spent thirty-five years in prison.

Security at Spain was tightened during Wallace's stay. Employees had to get new ID badges and couldn't get near the governor unless specifically involved in his rehabilitation. Wallace suffered some hearing loss after a bout with spinal meningitis when he was a young man, so he was also fitted with new hearing aids while at Spain. The audiology department took care of that procedure, but I didn't have security clearance to be anywhere near Wallace. However, there would be another opportunity to meet the governor.

Spain's administrators decided to hold a reception when his discharge became imminent so the governor could personally thank employees for his care. I, along with two friends from high school who also had summer jobs at Spain, got in the long line of hospital employees when the event began. There we all were, Black folks and white folks, waiting to shake the governor's hand.

There seemed to be no color distinctions as people chatted amiably about work and family and this and that. But then I started thinking about Wallace "standing in the schoolhouse door" to keep Black students out of the University of Alabama. I thought about his racist speeches, which helped light the fuse that emboldened the Ku Klux Klansmen who murdered the four Black girls killed when they dynamited the 16th Street Baptist Church. I even thought about Mama trying to find an empty alley where her four-year-old boy could relieve himself before peeing in his clothes because Wallace's vow of "segregation forever" prevented the child, and anyone else Black, from using a department store bathroom.

I thought about those things, and by the time I got within one hundred

CHAPTER 12

feet of the governor, sitting in his wheelchair, smiling, and shaking hands, Black and white, I knew I couldn't do it. I stepped out of the line and walked away, trying my best not to be noticed, not looking back at my friends. I wasn't making a political statement. I just wanted to leave the room. Maybe Wallace saw me, maybe he didn't. I didn't care.

Ironically, I interviewed Wallace several times a decade later as a reporter for United Press International. I never felt as though he treated me differently from white reporters. No matter who asked the question, if Wallace didn't want to answer it, his hearing aids always seemed to lose their effectiveness. I don't recall ever shaking Wallace's hand before an interview, or if he ever extended it to be shaken.

People still wonder if the assassination attempt made Wallace more receptive to Black people. Biographers say he had Black friends when he was growing up poor in Clio. You couldn't tell that by his politics, but he did moderate his tone when running for president and later when he needed Black votes to win a third term as Alabama's governor in 1982. Many Black Alabamians voted for him because they believed his promise to put more money in public education, which would help Black schools. Whether he was racist or not, I never regretted declining to shake Wallace's hand, and I never voted for him.

After my sophomore year at Baker, I was hired to be a cashier/dish washer at a full-service restaurant inside the huge Sears store in downtown Birmingham. I could tell the staff of mostly white servers and Black kitchen staff were amused to have a college boy working with them, but they were nice, and their occasional snickers when I got frustrated with a customer didn't bother me.

One of my first lessons was that restaurants are where some people go when they want to feel superior. They've taken orders all day at work, now they can give some. And when your job is to smile no matter what, you try to ignore their condescension, which can be hard when their food orders include a laundry list of demands rather than requests. "I want a steak that's medium, but no pink. If it's not right, I'm telling you now, I'm sending it back. And dressing to the side because y'all always overdress your salads. You hear me!"

Food was cooked to order, but customers ordered their items cafeteria-style from cashiers and waited for it before taking their seats. Sometimes the restaurant manager, Mr. Fowler, a short, rotund man who rarely smiled, would yell for me to quit the cash register and help wash dishes or mop the kitchen floor. After the dinner rush, he usually treated himself to a steak dinner and a large iced tea.

In the kitchen, the cooks and salad makers talked about their lives away from work and told me how proud of me they were of me for getting a college education. The kitchen was also a great place to be when too many sandwiches or desserts had been made and were given to the busboy and me. The white waitresses were nice too. They insisted on showing me the proper way to make Sears's signature milkshake, an orange whip. Even a college boy needs to learn skills that you can't get in a textbook but may come in handy when getting a job, they said.

After my junior year at Baker, I got a job making beds and mopping up blood and other ill-smelling stuff that I still don't like to think about as a housekeeper in Birmingham's Veterans Hospital. As unappealing as some aspects of that job were, I actually looked forward to putting on the blue shirts and pants that became my uniform and enjoyed my daily bus rides to the medical center complex at the University of Alabama in Birmingham. While the work was usually more tedious than hard, I learned some skills, including how to give sheets hospital corners when making beds.

The three other college students with summer jobs at the hospital and I often spent our time free time between tasks in the surgical intensive care unit, where the friendly nurses talked to us when they weren't busy. We liked the ICU because its patients were usually sedated and attached to catheters, which meant less mopping for us. The nurses keeping track of their patients' monitors let us help ourselves to Cokes while peppering us with questions about our schools, future plans, and girlfriends.

If you worked at a VA hospital in the 1970s, you were likely to be approached by someone who smoked and wanted you to buy them cigarettes, which back then were sold at discounted prices at stores within a federal government facility. Despite being a known carcinogen, tobacco wasn't banned from VA hospitals until 1991. Seems that "smoke 'em if you got 'em" attitude depicted in old war movies was hard to quit.

The VA's puffing patients included a pipe-smoking, always smiling, little old man who had a long gray beard and wore a red beret. The nurses said he was a veteran of the Spanish-American War, which was fought in 1898, but you couldn't tell that by his brisk walk. I never got a chance to talk to him but wondered about his age, what war stories he had to tell, and how he felt seeing the world change so much in his lifetime.

CHAPTER 13

TIME TO GET A REAL JOB

With more than enough credits to graduate, I took a home economics course during my final semester at Baker University, not just for fun but to improve my cooking skills. My roommates and I took turns preparing meals in our off-campus apartment, but I wanted to replicate some of Mama's home cooking. Once while frying chicken, I almost burned down our apartment when grease spattered onto our tiny kitchen's ancient wallpaper and ignited a fire. But no one succumbed to smoke inhalation, and remarkably the chicken was tasty, golden brown, and moist.

Only fifteen Black students were in Baker's 1975 graduating class of about one hundred. My girlfriend, Denice, had transferred to St. Francis School of Nursing in Wichita and a year later would receive both her RN degree from St. Francis and a BS from Baker. After being accepted by the graduate journalism schools at both Syracuse University and the University of Georgia, I instead went home and got a job interview with the state's largest newspaper, the *Birmingham News*.

Sadly, the only newspaper clips I had to show managing editor Jim Jacobson were of articles and opinion columns I had written for the *Orange*, Baker's student newspaper. I proudly handed him a copy of my favorite commentary for the *Orange*, comparing Baker's bucolic environment to "Sleep-Eze," saying the campus itself was a tranquilizing agent that put its students in such a stupor they blithely ignored what was wrong not only at Baker but also in the rest of the world. If "woke" had been a synonym for self-awareness in the 1970s, I would have used it to convey what I thought Baker students weren't.

I also showed Jacobson an article about shoplifting I wrote for Baldwin City's weekly newspaper, the *Ledger*. I wasn't proud of the article when I wrote it, thinking the assignment was rather dubious for the *Ledger*'s white editor in a virtually all-white town to give to a Black man. But it was the only example of professional experience I could show Jacobson.

"In a college town such as Baldwin, it is very easy to assume that most shoplifting is done by college students," I wrote. "Most of the town merchants, however, agree that most of the shoplifting cases in town involve the pre-teen and teenage residents of the community."

I believed the investigative journalism displayed in my article had destroyed a stereotype about Black people, but Jacobson wasn't impressed. He told me I wasn't ready for the *News*, but fortunately that wasn't the only path to possible employment in my hometown.

The *News*, which was owned by the Newhouse newspaper chain, had a joint operating agreement with the *Birmingham Post-Herald*, which was owned by Scripps-Howard. The two papers operated with separate staffs and newsrooms but on the same floor in the same building. The *News* owned the building, which was built in 1917, as well as the printing presses, and it employed the advertising and circulation staff for both papers.

Their papers' symbiosis meant that when Jacobson said he wouldn't hire me, I could walk down the hall and ask for a job interview with the *Post-Herald*'s top editor, Duard LeGrand, who was considered one of the most liberal newspaper editors in Alabama. When he retired in 1978, *Post-Herald* political reporter Ted Bryant described LeGrand in a tribute article as having "an acute and uncompromising sense of right and wrong. When public officials use their positions for personal gain, they are wrong where Duard is concerned. When they treat people with dark skin differently, they are wrong, purely, and simply."

LeGrand wrote columns in 1931 criticizing the unjust convictions of the "Scottsboro Boys"—nine young Black men sentenced to death for allegedly raping two white women who had been hitching a ride on the same freight train as the defendants. One of the accusers eventually recanted her testimony, but instead of releasing the innocent men, the state of Alabama would only commute their death sentences to life in prison.

While working for United Press International, I interviewed the last surviving

CHAPTER 13

Scottsboro Boy in 1983. Clarence Norris was granted parole in 1946 but violated it soon thereafter by leaving Alabama to live in New York. He remained there illegally for thirty years until George Wallace officially declared him "not guilty." With his conviction overturned, Norris sought compensation for the fifteen years he was in prison. "I was in jail for something I didn't do," he said during our telephone conversation. "They owe me something, whether I get it or not." The last Scottsboro Boy died in 1989, never receiving a penny of what he was owed.

I had been a *Post-Herald* reporter only three years when LeGrand died in 1978. I like to think maybe he had the Scottsboro Boys in mind when he hired me in 1975. I thus became the *Post-Herald*'s only Black reporter, but not its first. Its second was Adrienne Welch, who worked for the paper for two years before quitting six months after my arrival to work for United Press International in Atlanta. W. Arnett Bryant was the *Post-Herald*'s first Black reporter. He had a column called "Concerning Negroes" that, in the 1950s and '60s, covered virtually everything newsworthy in Birmingham's Black community.

Oscar Adams Sr. wrote a similar column for the *Birmingham News* called "What Negroes Are Doing" from 1918 until his death in 1946. Adams was succeeded by Geraldine Moore, who in 1964 was finally given the title "staff writer," a distinction previously reserved for white reporters. Ms. Moore was still reporting for the *News* when I became a cub reporter for the *Post-Herald* in 1975. She was still mostly covering the Black community, trying to make sure it was fairly depicted as more than a setting for crime and grime stories. I never took the opportunity to tell Ms. Moore how much I admired her for being a trailblazer. I should have. Ms. Moore died in 1987.

CHAPTER 14

NEWSROOMS WERE SMOKY AND LOUD

Newsrooms were in the final throes of a dying era when I became a reporter. You couldn't escape all the smoke puffed from cigars, cigarettes, and pipes in the *Post-Herald* newsroom in the mid-1970s. There were reporters who drank their lunch, or dinner, depending on the shift they worked. There were editors who kept a bottle in a desk drawer for "medicinal" purposes.

In that stimulating environment I learned almost as much about life as I did about journalism from veteran reporters including Bob Johnson, Bill Steverson, and Frank Morring, assistant state editor Mike Harris, and columnist Clettus Atkinson, a World War II Marine veteran who liked to brag that he kept his abdomen tighter than any of us younger men. Frank and Mike became lifelong friends despite our very different backgrounds. Frank was a prep school and Dartmouth College graduate. Mike, who graduated from public schools, was an Army veteran who served in Vietnam during the war.

The *Post-Herald* was a morning newspaper, so most of its reporters worked from 1:00 p.m. to 10:00 p.m. to make sure the papers the following day would have fresh news. There were only about twenty reporters, not including the sports staff, and probably half of us were under forty and unmarried. After work we typically had beers at one of several bars we frequented, including the Birmingham Press Club, which also served meals. Before heading home, I might stop by Frank's or Mike's apartment for a nightcap.

At Frank's we might end up discussing politics or philosophy. At Mike's

CHAPTER 14

we listened to jazz, mostly of the New Orleans variety. Leaving Mike's could be difficult. There was always one more record I "needed" to hear. If it wasn't Fats Domino, it was Professor Longhair. If it wasn't Dr. John, it was the Neville Brothers.

Probably our favorite bar was the Plaza, which had pinball machines and pool tables in the back. After a few beers Mike might put to use some of the billiards skills that he had honed in the Army. Mike rarely mentioned his time in the service except to fondly recall the "brothers," Black guys, who were his friends in Vietnam. But Mike was a shark—so good shooting pool that he sometimes asked me to be his partner knowing full well he might as well be asking a horse to swim. It didn't matter. Once it was Mike's turn to shoot, no one else got a chance. Cigarette dangling from his mouth, standing on the verge of inebriation, he was that good.

Some of the *Post-Herald*'s most colorful staff members seemed like characters from the Golden Age of newspapers depicted in movies like *Deadline U.S.A.*, *His Girl Friday*, and *The Front Page*.

There was Jack the Greek, our assistant news editor, one of the most magnanimous people you could ever meet, but his mood swings could be as abrupt as falling off a cliff. Conversely, "Thumbs Up," a copyeditor, never seemed to be in a bad mood, even when people made jokes about his being born without thumbs. "High-Pockets" George, a six-foot-three copyeditor, always wore trousers belted above his belly. And who could forget Charlie, another copyeditor, who, when he'd had enough drinks, might be persuaded to recite one of Hitler's speeches—in German.

Charlie and I once made a beer run after some of the *Post-Herald* staff met at his apartment after work. As we got out of the car, Charlie picked up a couple of toy machine guns that I didn't notice were on the back seat. Why he had toy guns, I never asked. Maybe they were props for one of the "blue" movies that I heard Charlie had made but never saw. So we grabbed the fake guns and nonchalantly walked into the nearby Western Supermarket—a Black man and a white man.

With several bars located near the grocery store, maybe its clerks were used to odd customers. No one called the cops. Toy guns in hand, we purchased our beer and walked out laughing. Imagine that happening amid today's more rampant gun violence.

Making white friends at the *Post-Herald* was easier than I thought it would be. My confidence was boosted every time I was invited to join a group for dinner or have a drink after work. We would joke, share dreams, get angry with each other, and, when needed, offer comfort. If I was struggling with a story, they offered advice.

It didn't take long for me to shed most of the Black militant–wannabe persona I had embraced in college, where I was one of our Black student union's leaders. But making friends at work wasn't the only reason I did that. I also needed to change my attitude to do my job. I discovered that not only do most people dislike talking to a reporter, but they also become more reluctant to speak when the reporter's skin color is different.

Watching photographers Bill Ingram, Jim Ware, Dennis Holt, and Tommy Langston helped me figure out how to get people being interviewed to open up. The photographers would chit-chat with cops while taking pictures and casually ask questions they knew their cub reporter needed answered. All I had to do was take good notes, which was good because I was just as reluctant to talk to police officers as they were to talk to me.

I still associated Birmingham's police with their former commissioner, Eugene "Bull" Connor, who a decade earlier sicced dogs on civil rights demonstrators. I wasn't comfortable talking to cops, but although he never showed it, Tommy may have had more reason to feel that way than I did. Police officers nonchalantly watched when Tommy was beaten by Ku Klux Klansmen on May 14, 1961, for taking photos of them attacking the Freedom Riders when they arrived at the Greyhound bus station.

"They grabbed the Rolleiflex and smashed the lens," Langston recalled in a 1984 interview for *Alabama Heritage* magazine. "I had a Minolta around my neck, and they grabbed the strap and nearly choked me to death. I just hit the ground and tried to cover my face. I think one of them was swinging a chain, because it caught me right across the face and broke my glasses. Then they started kicking me in the ribs. I don't know if they thought I was dead, but finally they stopped."

I eventually developed my own interview techniques and within months was getting the answers I needed not just from police officers but also from distraught people who had tragically lost a loved one, politicians who hated probing questions, even Ku Klux Klan members who loved publicity but didn't want to appear tolerant of Black people.

Leaving no stone unturned in my efforts to make white people feel comfortable being questioned by a Black man, I also toned down my style of dress by ditching colorful shirts and pants for what had become the unofficial standard

CHAPTER 14

uniform for reporters—blue shirt, khaki pants, dark blazer. Years later I was challenged by a group of Black high school students in Philadelphia who were interested in journalism careers. They felt I had gone too far in changing my appearance to make the white people I needed to interview feel comfortable.

"You should stay true to who you are," said one young lady. "I agree," I said. "But changing my wardrobe didn't change my truth. I am still a Black man. One day you may find out the difference in getting a job could be what you wear or maybe your hairstyle. That may not be fair, but it's a reality you should prepare for. And if you get that job, and do it well, what you wear or how you do your hair won't matter as much."

Talking to the high schoolers reminded me of my first days at the Post-Herald. Within a week, my first byline appeared on September 11, 1975. It was a feature story about a movie produced by the Alabama Committee for Humanities being filmed at the Greyhound bus terminal. I think our editor, Duard LeGrand, knew one of the cast members.

I still have a faded clip of that article, which includes a photograph of the cast in which I can be seen in the background. Reporters are not supposed to appear in news photos, so I don't know why my editors published this one. Maybe they wanted readers to see the *Post-Herald* had a Black reporter. Regardless, my colleagues laughed at me for making the rookie mistake of meandering into a photographer's frame.

Given my reluctance to interview police officers, I wasn't happy when I arrived late for work one afternoon only to have city editor Sid Thomas send me to a press conference with Police Chief James Parsons. Still feeling the aftereffects of a night out with some of my *Post-Herald* crewmates, I was mortified when Parsons invited me to take the only seat left in the room, which was close enough to smell his aftershave. I sat down, hoping I wouldn't belch the fragrance of stale beer. Adding insult to injury, the short briefing about some upcoming public relations event didn't even produce any information worthy of a story.

I had a lot of respect for Sid, who as a young reporter had covered corruption-plagued Phenix City, Alabama, where former state senator Albert Patterson was killed in a 1954 mob-style assassination shortly after running for attorney general. Sid and I got into a heated argument one day over a story I wrote that he refused to publish. I told Sid he never should have approved my request to cover a speech at the University of Alabama at Birmingham by Richard Lake, a Black activist also known as Mafundi who had spent time in prison.

Sid said he wasn't about to allow Mafundi to use the *Post-Herald* to make unsubstantiated claims of police terrorism and racism by public officials.

I argued that I had accurately reported comments made by a university-approved speaker at a UAB-sanctioned public event, but Sid wouldn't retreat. I saw it as one of those moments when a boss feels as if he needs to show his staff who is in charge. I knew better than to push the conversation further and retreated to my desk, angry but still employed.

After hearing Mafundi talk about racists in our midst, I couldn't help thinking that Sid was treating me like some uppity Negro he had to teach a lesson. But I stepped down from that perch a few months later when Sid showed his confidence in me by assigning me to run the city desk during my Sunday shift. I was essentially the Sunday city editor without the title, and as such, I had to edit stories and send them to the copy desk for their final editing and proofreading before publication. More importantly, it was my job to assign a reporter to any breaking news.

Less than three years out of college, and I had a newsroom management job. Recalling my argument with Sid, I decided it's better to be an editor giving orders than a reporter taking them. That's not to say I didn't enjoy reporting a big story, like the April 4, 1977, tornado that sped through several densely populated neighborhoods west of Birmingham. Twenty people were killed.

My sidebar to the paper's main story won a first-place newswriting award from the Associated Press in Alabama. My lede was simple. I let one of the tornado victims speak. "'I was sitting on my porch, and I could see it coming down the road,' said Curtis Eubanks, as he described the tornado that killed his next-door neighbor Monday. 'The children was all crying, and I just told them all to get into the hall. Nobody was hurt. It all happened so fast. They (tornadoes) don't sit around and talk. They come and go.'"

Let people tell their own stories became my motto. Another example is a 1979 article I wrote about Theodore Roosevelt Swain, a Black civilian worker who sued the Army after the brass at the Anniston Army Depot fired him for insubordination. Swain accused the Army of racism. "I've been called a communist, a troublemaker, and a smart-mouthed nigger," he said. "But I'll speak out against unjustness for the rest of my life. I don't intend to quit.... The system just doesn't approve of a Black man suing for his human rights."

That same year I wrote about John Snoddy, a white Army veteran who needed crutches to walk but was denied disability benefits after injuring his knee while stationed in Germany. Snoddy's comments more than forty years

CHAPTER 14

later sound like something that bubbled out of the same anti-government cauldron that Donald Trump dipped his ladle into to win the 2016 presidential election. "You think the Veterans Administration cares about that?" Snoddy fumed. He admitted writing bad checks to pay past-due bills but said he had no choice with the Army denying him what he felt he was owed. "You think they care about me losing my boat, about me not being able to take my boy fishing?"

People struggling like Snoddy were on my mind a dozen years later when I wrote an editorial for the *Birmingham News* titled "Bubba Has Brain," which criticized politicians who exploit Southerners' aversion to anything pertaining to "the government." The piece received the Alabama Press Association's "best editorial" award in 1992.

"You've probably heard of Bubba," the editorial read. "If memory serves correctly, his name first came up in Texas a while back and it resurfaced in Georgia just prior to this year's Democratic presidential primary. Bubba is the tag applied to the typical Southerner voter. He's supposed to be a conservative, working-class church goer with more common sense than schooling. He doesn't like politicians or taxes.

"Well, the politicians right now would have the rest of us believe Bubba is the reason they're struggling to put an acceptable tax package together. . . . Bubba isn't dumb; he knows the state has needs that cannot be met without better funding. But Bubba's not going to vote for new taxes unless he believes they are the result of the Legislature listening to him and not some lobbyist."

I wish I had as much confidence in today's Bubbas as I did back then. I still don't think the typical Southern voter is dumb, but some are guilty of willful ignorance. How else do you explain why so many supposedly conservative, working-class church goers support politicians like Donald Trump whose stances on taxes and spending are aimed at helping rich people, not everyday folks like them. They seem so enamored of politicians who say they will close the Mexico border, end abortion, and reverse gay rights that they don't notice what those politicians aren't saying—how they're going to unite our country.

CHAPTER 15

"LIVIN' LA VIDA LOCA" IN THE PROJECTS

My brother Calvin left home for the University of Iowa in 1975. That same summer I started work at the *Birmingham Post-Herald*. Like his older brothers, Calvin apparently also wanted to find adulthood without the restrictions that living with Mama imposed. She hated to see him go but was happy that at least one of her five sons would be with her in Loveman Village.

I thought about getting my own apartment but worried about the bite that would take out of my $135 a week salary, especially since I needed to buy a car to get around the city as a reporter. I bought a sleek, new silver-gray 1976 Chevrolet Monza, which almost immediately became my chariot not just for work but for adventure.

Mama took a risk by letting me stay with her in the projects. Technically, she was supposed to report my residency and the fact that I was now a working adult. But her subsidized rent was based on her meager Social Security checks, and if my salary were added to her Social Security income, the combined income would have made her ineligible to live in Loveman Village. By not even discussing that possibility, we risked having a neighbor snitch about our rule-breaking to Housing Authority officials. But to our knowledge, during the nearly two years I stayed with Mama, no one did.

The Loveman Village I lived in after college wasn't the same place I was brought home to as a baby twenty-two years earlier. I didn't give much thought to living in the projects when I was a child. Fights back then that might

CHAPTER 15

have ended with two guys cutting each other with knives were more likely in 1975 to end with gunfire. Drug use became so prevalent during those two decades since I was a baby that Mama routinely shooed people smoking marijuana off her back porch. Usually, the stoned trespassers were visiting our next-door neighbors, who always supported Mama's request that their friends move their rumps elsewhere.

Such respect largely resulted from Mama's having lived in the projects for so long. During that time, she became a reliable source of good advice and comfort for neighbors who needed a word of encouragement.

One woman confided in Mama that her husband was abusive, but it wasn't a secret. Everyone on our block could hear the woman and her two young daughters crying when Mr. Dave was beating her with his belt. To my knowledge, she never called the police, which was as typical then as it is now. So it seemed like poetic justice when Mr. Dave suffered a stroke or heart attack one day and died while sitting on the toilet.

Another woman who lived across the street from us in Loveman Village would occasionally knock on our back door when she had too much to drink. Mama wouldn't let Miss Bessie in if she was drunk but would talk to her through our screen door. One time I overheard Mama telling the woman she was better than the person she became when she was drunk.

Miss Bessie and Mama would have pleasant conversations inside our apartment when the woman was sober. Any recent intoxication was never discussed. They talked about their children, what they were cooking, and other people in the projects. Mama let Miss Bessie know she didn't think any less of her because of her alcoholism, and eventually I stopped seeing Miss Bessie drunk.

Mama's frank talks about drinking may have helped Miss Bessie, but she never confronted me about my late-night bar hopping. Most of the *Post-Herald* reporters' shifts ended at 10:00 or 11:00 p.m. to meet the morning newspaper's printing press deadlines, which was when we routinely headed to our favorite bar, the Plaza. Our crew usually included Frank Morring, Mike Harris, photographer Steve Gates, and sportswriter Bob Barnes. New reporters who joined our group later included Jeff Hardy, Joe Rassenfoss, and Jim Nesbitt, a rabid University of Tennessee football fan who kept his composure despite Alabama beating the Vols six times between 1975 and 1980.

I sometimes met Bob at his apartment for drinks on Saturday afternoons. I drank beers while Bob sipped screwdrivers barely diluted with orange juice. We chatted about work, maybe watched a ball game on TV, and sometimes drove to Lakeview Deli to hang out with its proprietor, Louie, who, between ringing up customers at the cash register, took sports bets over the phone. That was still illegal in the 1970s.

I drank more beers while listening to the bookie and Bob discuss ball games and life. After an hour or so, Bob and I might meet other friends from the *Post-Herald* for more drinks and eventually dinner. We liked Dugan's Pub and the Cadillac Café, a couple of popular restaurants on Birmingham's Southside. Their food was good and bars well-tended. After dinner we might head to the Plaza, which had pool tables and pinball machines in the back.

If it could have been bottled and sold, the Plaza's dive-bar ambiance might have made rich men of its owners, brothers Joe and Terry Cannon. But if we wanted live music, we might go to the Wooden Nickel bar to hear country rock bands covering songs by Asleep at the Wheel, Black Oak Arkansas, Jerry Jeff Walker, Lynyrd Skynyrd, and ZZ Top.

Some nights our last stop might be the Courtyard, a jazz club with tables set up outside a high-rise building, where its kitchen was located on the ground floor. Mike lived in an adjacent apartment building. So did Gary Mitchell, an AP reporter who one night begged us to help him move under the cloak of darkness so he could avoid a lease dispute with his landlord. Of course, we did it.

The Courtyard's house band was led by local legendary drummer Sherman Carson, also known as Foxxy Fats. The nightclub's clientele was always well integrated, which wasn't usually the case when I was with my white friends. But I never had a problem in the "New South" of the 1970s—not even when I walked into bars whose patrons proudly identified themselves as "redneck."

I enjoyed the music no matter where we partied and didn't hesitate when Frank invited me to join him and his friends at the annual Horse Pens 40 bluegrass festival on Chandler Mountain in St. Clair County. I was fond of bluegrass, having first heard it as a child when country music was about all anyone could get on the radio in Birmingham in the 1950s. Bar hopping with my *Post-Herald* friends, I became a fan of Three on a String, a popular bluegrass trio that performed at the Lowenbrau Haus, a pub located in the basement of the Jack 'n' Jill shoe store in Homewood.

The *Post-Herald* didn't have another Black reporter until Jeff Hardy was hired in 1979. Jeff and I quickly became friends, not out of necessity but because we liked each other. Jeff at first lived in a Southside apartment but then rented a house with another *Post-Herald* reporter, Joe Rassenfoss. Joe was one

CHAPTER 15

of those quick-witted guys who always seemed to have the perfect wise crack for any situation. Joe's yang to Jeff's yin produced some legendary house parties that even my wife, Denice, liked to attend.

There were times when Jeff and I ditched our white friends to see Black entertainers. Like when jazz organist Groove Holmes was doing two sets a night one weekend in the Gaston Motel's lounge. Groove was good, but he couldn't top B. B. King, who performed at a "cabaret" event at Boutwell Auditorium. Cabaret meaning it was a BYOB affair, with tables and chairs set up around the stage. You had to bring your own liquor and purchase a "set-up," which was a paper bucket filled with ice and four plastic cups.

The audience put on almost as good a show as B. B. We got into the groove watching people shout encouragement at the musicians while trying to dance without bumping into people sitting at the tightly arranged tables.

Boutwell Auditorium was also where I saw the Grateful Dead in 1978 after being assigned at the last minute to cover the band's concert. That was after the *Post-Herald*'s entertainment reporter, Emmett Weaver, unexpectedly decided a rock concert was outside the parameters of his artistic knowledge. It's still hard to believe I was paid to see the Dead. Almost immediately upon entering Boutwell, I saw several of my *Post-Herald* drinking mates. No wonder none of them were available to review the concert.

Despite temptation, I didn't get caught up in the moment and delivered my review both on time and in very little need of editing. "Some rock groups just aren't as good as their hyped-up reputations," it began. "A lot of groups find it hard to warm up a crowd and then keep it excited through an entire act. But the Grateful Dead are not your everyday, high voltage, rock-and-roll band, and they aren't about to let anyone forget it.

"The Dead were in complete control of its first-ever Birmingham concert last night at Boutwell Auditorium.... The crowd included quite a few youngsters who may have some difficulty appreciating what Haight-Ashbury was all about ... [but the] band received a standing ovation from the moment it began until the last song."

After starting work at the *Post-Herald*, I also began hanging out with a group of Black guys I had known since elementary school. We had never been close friends as boys, but as adults, and without Mama's tight reins getting in the way, we enjoyed each other's company. The fellows seemed amused by my being less of a nerd.

Robert Murray, who also still lived with his parents, usually hosted our gatherings. We would drink wine and beer and talk about sports, women, cars, and old times. It was almost like dorm life at Baker, except we weren't stuck on a college campus. Occasionally, we would check out a house party or a Black nightclub like Samson & Delilah's.

I worked Sundays through Thursdays at the *Post-Herald*, so Thursday nights were the beginning of my weekends, and I rarely made it home before the clocks said it was Friday. But Mama never uttered more than a hint at breakfast, which she always served, that I needed to be careful. Thank God the prayers I know she said for me were much more fervent. I have no doubt that those prayers saved me more than once, like the night I slammed on the brakes driving home on a rain-slick street and stopped only a body's length from a telephone pole.

Years later after Calvin's death, I wondered if Mama had treated him differently when he was home from college and stayed out late. Did Mama worry more about Calvin because he was gay? He never admitted his homosexuality until he was dying and only did so then because a friend told me without his knowledge. But I think Mama suspected it. After all, she and Calvin lived alone together most of the four years I was away in college.

I suspected it, too, but never said anything to Calvin, not wanting anything to affect the close relationship we both tried to maintain since childhood.

I was four years older than Calvin but always felt closer to him than my other brothers, even Don, who was only eighteen months older than me. Somehow, Calvin and I always seemed more in sync. He was more than a brother; he was my friend. We grew up trading insults, sharing inside jokes, and making up nicknames for some of the memorable characters who also lived in Loveman Village.

I think Mama wanted to cling to the image she had of Calvin as a child too. She knew Calvin's homosexuality was then against the law in Alabama and other states that made being gay a crime. Such laws weren't struck down by the US Supreme Court until 2003, long after Calvin was dead.

But more so than the ramifications, Mama was likely worried about how Calvin would be treated by people who knew our family if his homosexuality was revealed. She likely thought about Roger, the gay son of her friend Marie King, a hairdresser. Roger was both routinely ridiculed and beaten up for perming his hair, dressing flamboyantly, and mimicking a woman's soft voice.

Mama didn't want that to happen to Calvin. Neither did I. Sometimes when I thought about Calvin I thought about a man, rumored to be gay, who

CHAPTER 15

taught Sunday school at our church when I was a child. Westminster Presbyterian's largely middle-class members proudly labeled our services "dignified." But one Sunday, this always impeccably dressed gentleman arrived at church with visible bruises on his face, and it was whispered that he had been in a fight with his male partner.

Imagine Westminster folk whispering about Calvin. I think that possibility played a large role in his deciding not to come home after he graduated from the University of Iowa. Mama taught her boys to never embarrass the family, so he moved to San Francisco.

I should have been as concerned about embarrassing my family with my late nights out, but I wasn't. At least not right away. But after nearly two years of living dangerously while staying with Mama in the projects, my lifestyle began to lose its attractiveness. I began to admit I was still more of a bookworm than a barfly and decided it was time to reduce my treadmill's speed. To do that, though, I needed help. Marriage had always been my intention, so why not now? Why not ask Denice to marry me? We still considered ourselves a couple, but long-distance relationships aren't always as solid as either participant thinks it is. It was time for us to find out about ours.

ABOVE

Janye Jackson (*second from right*), Harold Jackson's mother, age eighteen, attending a fundraiser ball in 1924 for the cosmetology school she attended in Birmingham, Alabama.

LEFT

Lewis Jackson, Harold Jackson's father, a truck driver for R. B. Broyles Furniture Co. in Birmingham, Alabama, dressed up for this studio photo taken in 1950. He was forty-one years old.

LEFT

Harold Jackson, age six, in a student photo taken in 1959 when he was in first grade at Center Street Elementary School in Birmingham, Alabama.

RIGHT

Harold Jackson, age three, posed for a snapshot in 1956 with his five-year-old brother Don, and neighbor Mabel Jean Harris, in the Loveman Village housing project in Birmingham, Alabama.

LEFT

Janye Jackson, recently widowed, poses in her home in the Loveman Village housing project in Birmingham, Alabama, with sons (*left to right*) Harold, Calvin, Anthony, and Don.

ABOVE

Calvin Jackson (*right*) visiting his brother Jeffery in Portland, Oregon, in 1978. Jeffery moved to Portland several years earlier after graduating from the University of Washington.

RIGHT

Harold Jackson (*top row, first person left*) was among the fifteen Black students who graduated in 1975 from Baker University in Baldwin, Kansas. Founded in 1858, Baker is the oldest four-year college in the state.

BELOW

Harold Jackson (*top row, second person right*), was inadvertently included in this news photo of a police brutality protest he covered in 1976 for the *Birmingham Post-Herald*. So was TV news reporter Larry Langford (*bottom, right*), who thirty years later was elected Birmingham's mayor.

ABOVE

Harold Jackson (*seated*) in a 1982 photo with Joey Ledford, United Press International's state editor for Alabama. Jackson replaced Ledford in that position in 1983.

LEFT

Harold Jackson (*left*), Ron Casey, and Joey Kennedy celebrate in the Birmingham News newsroom after learning they had won the 1991 Pulitzer Prize for editorial writing.

ABOVE

Harold Jackson (*left*) had been editorial page editor for the *Philadelphia Inquirer* for nine years when he was captured in this 2016 photo sharing a joke with his deputy editor, Josh Gohlke.

RIGHT

Harold Jackson and his wife, Denice, participated in a Habesha coffee ceremony in 2010 in Addis Ababa, Ethiopia. Denice, a registered nurse, was part of a medical mission that Harold wrote about for the *Philadelphia Inquirer*.

LEFT

Harold Jackson (*right*) being greeted by the local Communist Party official outside the municipal office building for Da Ping, a tiny village of about one hundred residents on Mount Huashan in China.

ABOVE

Harold Jackson (*right*) interviewing Democratic presidential candidate Barack Obama, who was seeking the *Philadelphia Inquirer*'s endorsement for the 2008 Pennsylvania primary election.

CHAPTER 16

STEPPING INTO MATRIMONY

The little time Denice and I spent together after I graduated from Baker University could be counted in days, not weeks. We both started college as freshmen at Baker in 1971, but when she became a junior, Denice began a two-year program at the St. Francis School of Nursing, 160 miles away in Wichita, Kansas.

I could afford the Greyhound bus ride to see Denice only a few times before I graduated from Baker in 1975 and moved home to Birmingham. I flew to Wichita for her graduation in 1976, and she visited me once after that in Birmingham. Otherwise, long-distance phone calls were the extent of our relationship. Even so, we thought of ourselves as a pair.

We would talk on the phone about Denice's work as a nurse at Menorah Medical Center in Kansas City and mine as a reporter for the *Post-Herald*. We talked about old times at Baker, its teachers and former classmates. We talked about our families, who had a new job, a new baby, or was sick. We talked about work, what we liked about it, what we hated, who we hated. We talked about going out with friends, never mentioning anyone who might be a romantic rival. But we never talked about marriage.

Thinking maybe I shouldn't even pop the question, I decided I needed advice. My best friend, Charles Abron, would have been my first choice for that. But he was somewhere on a Navy ship. So I sought counsel from my closest friend from the *Post-Herald*, Frank Morring. Frank was the only one of my

CHAPTER 16

white coworkers whom I ever brought to my home in the projects. He was the only one to meet Mama.

Once, after noticing Mama and me casually conversing in a less formal vernacular than we might otherwise use around white folks, Frank said, "Harold, you speak two languages." I just smiled but thought to myself, "Right, English and Ebonics." Black sociologist W. E. B. DuBois got it right when he said more than a century ago that African Americans are residents of two nations, one inside the other.

I decided to ask Frank about my marrying Denice one night when we were drinking beers at Dugan's Pub. I asked Frank point blank if I should propose to Denice, and he abruptly turned as shy as a farm boy being asked to escort the queen of a debutante ball. I didn't expect that from this typically articulate graduate of Indian Springs School and Dartmouth College. But I think I understood Frank's hesitation.

Denice lived in Kansas City, not Birmingham, so he hadn't been able to observe us as a couple. I could see him not wanting to be an accomplice to what might eventually become a failed marriage. Or maybe, having gotten to know me quite well, Frank didn't think I was ready for marriage.

I tried to explain my love for Denice.

I told Frank her personality was such that I didn't know anyone who didn't like her. I said I knew she would be a good nurse because she always seemed able to put people she came in contact with at ease. Denice seemed able to sense what other people were feeling and instinctively knew what to say or do to make them feel comfortable. I told him that was especially so with me, that being with her made me happy.

Frank advised me to follow my heart. I told him I would, went home, and found a box of old school papers in my bedroom closet that included a poor attempt at a poem inspired by Denice, which I never shared with her.

> **By My Side**
> If I could have one wish, one desire,
> It would be to have you by my side.
> Knowing you were my constant companion,
> Would mean everything; heighten my pride.
> A love like this that I have for you,
> Could never diminish, only grow.

So, let us always be by each other's side,
True happiness is holding you close.

Yes, corny, but since I've opened the door, here's a poem I wrote after learning "seeing the elephant" was a nineteenth-century expression for wanting to see all the world could offer.

Ambition
I want to see the elephant; the strange, the bizarre.
I want to see all the things that make men travel far.
Distant voyages I seek; I would climb the heights.
Ordinary days are not for me; adventure is my light.

Mama seemed more concerned than happy when I told her I wanted to marry Denice. I figured that having gone through a divorce before marrying Daddy, she didn't want me to make the same mistake. Also, with Calvin away in college, my moving out would leave her alone. She had only met Denice once when she came to Birmingham to visit us nearly a year earlier. But Mama gave our prospective marriage her blessing, probably concluding, as I had, that I needed to settle down.

So I bought the best wedding ring set I could afford from Birmingham's best jewelry store, Bromberg's, and a few weeks later drove the seven hundred miles to Kansas City. I stayed with Ricky, my former Baker roommate who didn't return to Washington, DC, after graduating. Rickey's tiny second-floor apartment was in a neighborhood that made me fear someone would rob me of the engagement ring I had bought. But I was nervous for nothing. A day after my arrival I proposed, and Denice said yes.

Less than a year later, we were married in Kansas City at Swope Park Church of Christ, with Pastor Marion Holt Sr. officiating. Denice had handled all the arrangements, including a booze-free reception at the church. Calvin flew in from Iowa City to be my best man, the only one of my relatives to make it, but Calvin represented our family well. He and I stayed at Denice's cousin Bud's house for two nights prior to the wedding. Ricky and I spent school holidays with Bud when we didn't have the money to fly home. His mother, Clara Mae Mays, treated us no differently than the three sons she had.

Denice and I spent one "honeymoon" night in a swanky Kansas City hotel

CHAPTER 16

before loading up and driving back to Birmingham. We stayed with Mama for about a month before moving into a one-bedroom apartment in Homewood, a Birmingham suburb south of the city. It was the first time since arriving home from St. Vincent's Hospital as an infant that my home address wasn't in the Loveman Village housing project.

CHAPTER 17

CAN'T FEED A FAMILY ON PEANUTS

It didn't take long for Denice to be hired as a registered nurse in the University of Alabama at Birmingham medical center. I thought I was doing fine at the *Post-Herald* until about a year after I was hired when our editor, Duard LeGrand, was diagnosed with cancer. Scripps-Howard, the newspaper chain that owned the *Post-Herald*, chose Angus McEachran, an assistant managing editor at the Memphis *Commercial Appeal*, to replace Duard, who died in 1978.

Angus brought his reputation as a belligerent taskmaster with him to Birmingham, and it didn't take long for him to let me know he wasn't satisfied with my work. I was taken aback by his dismissiveness. Having in three years moved from general assignment to education reporter to covering city hall during Richard Arrington Jr.'s successful run to become Birmingham's first Black mayor, I felt I had proved my mettle.

I had cultivated reliable sources inside city hall and developed noteworthy relationships with council members that had produced some solid stories. Angus wasn't impressed. One day he called me into his office to tell me I was being reassigned. I thought the real problem was my race, that Angus didn't trust a Black man to impartially cover a Black mayor.

He reassigned me to cover health, which was an important beat in a city where the medical industry had replaced US Steel as its biggest employer. But after covering the political intrigue inside city hall, covering doctors and hospitals seemed boring. There was also the fact that Denice worked for the city's

CHAPTER 17

biggest hospital, UAB, which raised the potential for conflicts of interest. But I didn't want to give my new boss any reason to dislike me more than he already seemed to, so I never argued with him about my new assignment.

In time I actually began to enjoy the beat. Instead of parsing politics, I was writing about the dramatic expansion of Birmingham's sixty-block medical center, innovative medical and other scientific research at UAB, labor issues involving staff beyond doctors and nurses, and, best of all, health-related features that allowed people to tell their own stories, stories like three-year-old Billy McDougal's battle with leukemia.

"I was afraid, I was terrified," said Billy's mother in my article describing her reaction to her son's diagnosis only months after his birth. "I thought that was it. He would just last a few weeks and that would be it." But with chemotherapy and radiation treatment, Billy survived and was as normal as any other three-year-old boy when I interviewed his mother.

But not even my enjoyment in telling stories like Billy's could erase my frustration with the *Post-Herald*'s poor pay. With Denice and me expecting our first child, I wasn't making much more than the $135 a week I started with four years earlier. Looking for better pay, I applied for a communications job with Alabama's newly elected US senator, Howell Heflin.

I thought my interview with the senator went well, but someone else had an inside track. Heflin instead hired Mary E. Stansel, a young lawyer who had worked with U. W. Clemon. In 1980, Heflin successfully nominated Clemon to become Alabama's first Black federal judge. Stansel became famous in her own right in 1994 when she accused NAACP executive director Benjamin F. Chavis Jr. of sexual harassment. The NAACP board fired Chavis after learning that he used $332,000 of the organization's money without asking to settle the case.

Not getting the Heflin job bothered me, but as the old saying goes, one door closing doesn't mean another won't open. Carole Corlew, a United Press International reporter in Birmingham, told me she was being transferred to a different bureau and that I should apply to replace her. I don't remember hugging her but could have.

Carol was dating Frank Morring at the time and often joined our crew that met regularly at the Plaza or other bars after work. Based on her recommendation and what I think was a good interview, I was hired by UPI's Alabama news editor, Rick Beene. A few months later, Denice and I had our first child, Annette. Fifteen months later, our son Dennis was born in 1981.

UPI's offices were in the back of the *Post-Herald*'s sprawling newsroom, which prompted its news editor, Jimmy Goodloe, to joke that I had to walk only a few hundred feet to get a better paycheck. But there was nothing funny about the newspaper's meager salaries.

The *Post-Herald*'s newsroom staff threatened to strike before I was hired by UPI, but we were terrified to go through with it in a right-to-work state like Alabama. That meant there weren't any laws that gave workers the right to unionize. Not wanting to risk being fired, we instead held protest rallies and, in retrospect, dumbly asked readers to boycott our income source. During one protest, we tossed bags of peanuts to people from a moving flatbed truck and held up signs that said "The *Post-Herald* Pays Us Peanuts."

We thought the Newspaper Guild might help us, but with fewer than fifty reporters, photographers, and editors who would qualify to be represented by the union for journalists, the guild said our group needed to be larger to become a chapter.

Fortunately for us, the printers' union wasn't as discriminating. It said our size didn't prohibit us from becoming an International Typographical Union (ITU) "chapel," which was the term ITU applied to units whose members didn't perform the actual work of printers. So, with the union's blessing, that's what we did.

My brief stint as a ITU member before joining UPI allowed me to brag years later that I was among the rare breed of journalists who had been members of both the writers and printers newspaper unions. Computerization put the ITU out of business in 1986, as composing room jobs faded away. The death of newspapers nationwide as digital replaces print has made the guild's future murky as well.

UPI's higher pay was hard earned. Rick, Kurt Franck, and I worked long shifts in the Birmingham bureau, taking turns starting either at 5:00 a.m. or 1:00 p.m. and ending when there was no more news to file to the wire. A phone call from UPI's regional headquarters in Atlanta to the bureau or our homes at any time of the day or night might send one of us to whatever corner of Alabama had big news happening. When we couldn't get there in time, we hired stringers from local newspapers, radio, or TV stations to cover stories until we could.

Orbie Medders, UPI's Alabama sales representative in Alabama, also had office space in the Birmingham bureau. His job was to keep the newspapers, TV, and radio stations that subscribed to our service happy.

CHAPTER 17

Rick was promoted and transferred in 1981, and Joey Ledford became Alabama news editor. When Joey was similarly promoted in 1983, I succeeded him and became boss of a Birmingham staff that included Kurt and Mark Harris, who was later replaced by Phil Jenkins. In addition to those of us in Birmingham who covered news all over Alabama, my staff included political reporters Bessie Ford, Bob Lowry, and Jeff Woodard in Montgomery; news reporter Dana Beyerle in Huntsville; and David Tortorano, who covered the Alabama/Florida side of the Gulf Coast from Pensacola.

Our goal was simple. Beat the Associated Press in reporting breaking news so newspapers and broadcast outlets would use our work instead of theirs. My biggest win as state editor was when we beat the AP in reporting the death of legendary University of Alabama football coach Paul "Bear" Bryant on January 27, 1983. Bryant died just six weeks after he announced his retirement following what for him had been a disappointing 8–4 season.

I was the only Black reporter at Bryant's retirement news conference, though you wouldn't know I was there from looking at a photograph of the event, which I didn't see until decades later when it was posted on a Facebook page. Only white faces appeared in that record of a special moment in sports history. No one told me to stick around after the press conference to be photographed with the coach and other sports writers who had covered his games.

Maybe that was an unintended slip-up by the university's sports information office. But having covered other sports events in Alabama for UPI where I was the only Black reporter, including NASCAR races and PGA tournaments, I'm not so sure. I didn't worry much at the time about being slighted because of my race. I was too caught up in meeting each day's unexpected challenges. UPI staffers, or "Unipressers," as we liked to be called, used the word "wired" to describe our anxiousness to take on the next big story. But our eagerness faded when UPI's financial struggles one day left us with paychecks that bounced. With the company facing bankruptcy, I knew it was time to find another job, and luckily, a former *Post-Herald* staffer opened the right door. Charles "Chas" Chamberlain left Birmingham a year or two earlier to be a graphic artist for the *Philadelphia Inquirer*. I was hesitant when he suggested I apply for a job there, but the possibility of working for one of America's greatest newspapers enticed me.

I spoke on the phone with Jeff Price, the *Inquirer*'s newsroom recruiter, who arranged for me to take Knight Ridder's copyeditor test at the chain's nearest newspaper, the *Columbus Enquirer*, which was 170 miles from Birmingham in Georgia. I didn't do great on the test, but my UPI background caught the eye of *Inquirer* national editor Lois Wark, who hired me to be an assistant national editor, joining a staff that included David Taylor, Herb Kestenbaum, Ashley Halsey, and Jan Schaffer.

The *Inquirer* paid for a house-hunting trip for Denice and me, but given only a few days to look, we didn't see anything we liked. Being from the South and Midwest, we weren't familiar with Philadelphia's rowhouse neighborhoods. Even nice middle-class homes were often connected as "twins" or duplexes and had small yards that reminded me of the "garden" apartments housing project where I grew up.

We decided Denice would remain in Birmingham with our two children while I began my new job in Philly and looked for a place for our family to reunite as soon as possible. Denice got the worse part of that deal; she had to work her shifts at University Hospital—which meant leaving work to pick up Annette and Dennis from their preschool at Southside Baptist Church—cook, clean, and otherwise maintain our home while trying to keep our kids' spirits up during my absence.

I worked what newspapers, back when they published multiple editions, called the "lobster shift," which for me was 6:00 p.m. to 1:00 a.m., Sunday through Thursday. My first day was a great introduction to life in Philly. After parking my Volvo wagon in a nearby lot, I walked less than a block to *Inquirer*, only to find a small group of mostly Black men standing outside and holding signs indicating they were protesting wage issues.

Being from Alabama, a right-to-work state where even the steelworkers rarely hit the streets, the possibility of being harassed for crossing a picket line never entered my mind. I simply walked past the assembled men and entered the *Inquirer* building, eager to begin my new job. No one said anything to me. No one tried to stop me, so I thought nothing of it until the next day, when I found a greeting card that had been placed on my desk by the paper's deputy managing editor, Jim Naughton, who wrote a brief note thanking me for being dedicated enough to walk past the picket line.

That made me happy, but the feeling didn't last. The wildcat strike was by porters and janitors who had been working without a contract for a year. Remembering our labor struggles at the *Post-Herald*, I regretted having crossed their picket line and was thankful that the protesters had let an unwitting scab cross unharmed. At least the one-day strike was successful. The union and

CHAPTER 17

Inquirer came to a quick agreement, likely because it didn't want the Teamsters Union, which was honoring the porters and janitors' strike, to stop delivering papers.

That happy ending provided no indication of the much more consequential union activity I would face later.

CHAPTER 18

EVERY DAY'S A CHALLENGE IN PHILLY

After the Inquirer told me it would no longer pay for the room in a very nice hotel I stayed in for two weeks after starting my new job in Philadelphia, I moved into a drab but clean, less expensive room at the Parker Spruce Hotel near the University of the Arts. The hotel offered weekly rates, but my stay didn't last that long. Quiet the morning I moved in, that night served up an unending cacophony of banging doors and stomping feet as its other, now more visible residents came and went.

"Sounds like a hot-sheets joint," said my boss, Lois Wark, when I described my new home away from home. I had figured that out, too, and knew I needed to move fast. I sought help from Acel Moore, the *Inquirer*'s associate editor whom I first met five years earlier when he spoke to the Birmingham Association of Black Journalists. Acel won a Pulitzer Prize for investigative reporting in 1977 and was a founding member of the National Association of Black Journalists (NABJ).

After hearing my plight, Acel made a quick call to someone he knew at Temple University, and just like that I was provided a room to rent in its nursing school dormitory. The dorm was tidy and quiet, especially on weekends when most of its other residents seemed to disappear. For me, it was like an oasis in the dicey North Philadelphia neighborhood where it was located. Crack dealers and junkies were everywhere.

Fearing my Volvo wagon would be stolen, I kept it parked in a lot across

CHAPTER 18

the street from the *Inquirer* and took either the bus or the subway to and from work. That's how I learned mass transit etiquette, which in Philly in the 1980s meant to never look anyone in the face and, unless you're screaming for help, to keep your mouth shut.

I drove the Volvo only on weekends to house hunt. It took months before I believed I had found a place suitable for my young family. It was a newly built three-floor, three-bedroom townhouse apartment in the city's affluent Chestnut Hill neighborhood, which was also where Mayor Frank Rizzo lived. The rent was higher than I wanted to pay, but the suburban feel of the community seemed like the right setting for our children. Annette, five, started kindergarten at John Story Jenks Elementary School, and Dennis, four, went to the preschool just across Germantown Avenue at St. Paul's Episcopal Church.

With Denice working a morning shift at Temple University Hospital, I would walk the kids both to and from school. Heading home, we often stopped to buy a snack at the commuter train station. Then I would play with the kids, watch TV with them, and maybe prepare a meal so Denice wouldn't have to when she came home. Her shift ended at 3:00 p.m. She usually got home by 4:00, which left little time before I had to leave for work. That was hard, and Philadelphia didn't seem as family friendly as Birmingham, but we were happy because we were together. Unfortunately, that happiness didn't last.

On September 7, 1985, the nine unions representing all of the *Inquirer*'s and *Philadelphia Daily News*'s 4,774 workers went on strike. There would be no casual walking across picket lines this time. The strike lasted forty-six days. That was seven weeks of me not working or getting paid. I had to ask my brother Anthony for help to pay our bills.

Meanwhile, Denice was having her own work-related problems. Temple University Hospital hired her to be a nurse manager, but labor and management were like water and oil in Philadelphia in the 1980s; they didn't mix. Denice's friendly demeanor failed to melt the cold hearts of some of the management-phobic nurses she was supposed to supervise. Months after taking the job, Denice left Temple for a less frustrating but lower-paying staff nurse position at Germantown Hospital. That's when we started talking about going back to Alabama. Then came news that Mama had suffered a fall at home, nothing serious but concerning nonetheless.

Mama lived in the small three-bedroom house we left when we moved to Philadelphia in 1985. It was our first house, having moved there in 1980 after living in apartments our first three years of marriage. I was so happy to get

Mama out of the projects. She was seventy-one and had lived in Loveman Village for nearly thirty-five years. She lived alone. The closest one of her five sons was Anthony, and he lived eighty-five miles away with his family in Eutaw. I felt she needed someone closer in case another fall or something more tragic occurred.

I reached out to the *Birmingham News*'s editor, Jim Jacobson, who twelve years earlier as managing editor turned me down for a *News* job because I lacked experience. This time he was more receptive, and after we corresponded for several weeks by letter and telephone, Jim offered me a job as an assistant city editor. The pay was slightly less than what I made in Philadelphia, but the cost of living was also lower. Meanwhile, Denice returned to University Hospital, where she eventually became an operating room nurse.

I worked under city editor Randy Henderson, an outstanding journalist and one of the most even-tempered newspapermen I'd ever met. Nothing fazed Randy, but at times the higher pitch of his voice betrayed his emotion. Under my direct supervision were religion writer Greg Garrison and health and science reporters John Mangels, Bob Blalock, and Jeff Hansen, who had a PhD in microbiology. Their consistently good story ideas and near flawless copy made my job easy. Only occasionally did I edit stories by Black reporters Ingrid Kindred, Sherrel Wheeler Stewart, Solomon Crenshaw, and Eddie Lard. Nathan Turner, who I had known since elementary school, was a copyeditor. Their hard work made me proud just to know them.

Less often, I edited Rick Bragg, who later won a Pulitzer Prize at the *New York Times*. Rick so vividly described people and places that his friends teased him by annually presenting a "Torn Lampshade" award to the *News* reporter who wrote the most colorfully worded story. The prize's name was a reference to Rick's lede to a 1986 story about an unsolved murder, which began, "Night comes to Birmingham like a thin, torn lampshade over a bright, hot bulb, unable to snuff the light out completely but enough to cast pockets of shadow here and there."

When there was an opening on the *News* editorial board less than two years into my job as assistant city editor, I immediately asked Ingrid Kindred for advice. One of its first Black reporters, Ingrid had been with the *News* seventeen years. She would know if I had a legitimate shot at getting the job. Ingrid was both a mentor and a friend. She would invite me to join her and other Black professionals she knew for happy hour drinks after work. Saying Denice and I needed to be more active socially, she also invited us to the annual balls held by her sorority, Alpha Kappa Alpha.

CHAPTER 18

Ingrid advised me to apply for the editorial board opening, and with that encouragement, I did. I was asked by Tom Scarritt, who had succeeded retired editorial page editor James McAdory, to write a sample editorial. Told to choose any topic, I decided it would be too predictable to choose race relations, so I instead wrote a piece about how the dangerous chlorofluorocarbons being used as propellants in aerosol sprays were endangering human existence on our planet by intensifying global warming. Scarritt hired me, and I became the *News*'s first Black editorial writer.

That distinction brought to mind the late Emory O. Jackson, who sixteen years earlier, when I was a high school senior, presented me with a college journalism scholarship from the National Newspaper Publishers Association and Coca-Cola USA. As editor of the *Birmingham World*, Jackson wrote editorials that helped lay the groundwork for segregation's demise in Alabama's largest city. I wondered how much he would have accomplished if he had been given the opportunity I now had to reach a larger, more diverse readership. I wanted to similarly represent a distinctly Black viewpoint when writing about my community.

Also on the board were Ron Casey, who wrote editorials too, and our cartoonist, Mark Cullum. Jacobson, as editor, and our publisher, Victor Hanson II, were listed as board members but typically didn't get involved unless we were making an important political endorsement or writing about a major advertising client—that is, except for the time Hanson objected to a column that I had written about the upcoming twenty-fifth anniversary of the Selma to Montgomery march.

This was after Scarritt had been promoted to executive editor and Ron succeeded him as editorial page editor. After seeing a preview copy of my column before it was published, Hanson told Casey he thought my vivid descriptions of state troopers beating the civil rights demonstrators trying to cross the Edmund Pettus Bridge were inflammatory and unnecessary. Casey asked me if I would be willing to remove those descriptions, and I told him no, that the troopers' brutality was what should be remembered most.

Hanson never spoke to me directly, so my reaction to his objections was based solely on Ron's relayed expression of the publisher's objections. I didn't feel his complaint was sufficient enough to censor my work, and even though I feared being fired, I pleaded for the column to be printed as written. Ron and Jacobson both spoke with Hanson, but several hours passed before I got the good news that he had relented.

The "Bloody Sunday" marchers included John Lewis, who I would later meet at a NABJ convention in Washington, DC, in 1998. The Georgia congressman was born in Pike County, Alabama, which was where my mother was also was born. He was chairman of the Student Nonviolent Coordinating Committee when he led marchers on "Bloody Sunday" in Martin Luther King Jr.'s absence. We chatted at the NABJ convention as he autographed my copy of his memoir, *Walking With the Wind*, which describes better than I ever could in a column what Hanson didn't want me to mention.

State troopers both mounted and on foot attacked the marchers when they refused orders to disperse. Lewis said he will never forget the sounds of horses' hooves and troopers' boots striking the hard asphalt of the highway while a raucous crowd of white onlookers urged the troopers to beat the demonstrators. "Get the niggers," shouted one woman. Lewis said he felt no pain when a husky state trooper swung a baton that struck his head and left him dazed. He said he fell to the ground but never passed out, even after a second blow, instead collecting vivid memories that he never wanted to forget.

CHAPTER 19

WEREN'T TRYING TO WIN A PULITZER

After Tom Scarritt became the *News*'s executive editor in 1989, Ron Casey was promoted to editorial page editor and Joey Kennedy, a reporter, took Casey's place as an editorial writer. The three of us worked well together, grinding out editorials and taking turns writing columns for a feature we called Friday Forum. Then in 1990, when the state legislature blatantly bowed down to special interests by trying to delay publication of a special committee's report on Alabama's discriminatory tax system, we began a special project that, to our amazement, won a Pulitzer Prize.

For decades, high taxes paid by poor and middle-class families had subsidized the lucrative tax breaks Alabama gave to powerful corporations, agribusinesses, and timber companies. Since the state's legislators wouldn't admit that to the public, we decided to do it for them by issuing our own report.

We spent months talking to historians and economists who explained how the tax system had evolved into the monstrosity it had become. We visited communities hurt by a tax system that inadequately funded public schools and aid to the poor, and we pointed out that farmers got tax breaks to buy feed for calves, while mothers buying formula did not.

Our series of eight editorials was published under the title "What They Won't Tell You about Your Taxes." We explained how Alabama's lowest-per-capita tax rate in the country underfunded those state services most needed by the poor. For example, a family of three could not earn more than $1,400 a year

WEREN'T TRYING TO WIN A PULITZER

to qualify for public assistance, and foster families were paid less to take care of abused children than a typical kennel charged to board a dog.

I wrote three editorials, including "Nickels and Dimes," which detailed how Alabama used its regressive sales tax to overburden the poor and middle class while giving overly generous tax breaks to corporations, and "Handcuffing Money," which criticized the state's excessive use of a process called "earmarking" that allowed politicians to spend tax money where they wanted instead of in areas where it was most needed, like Alabama's terribly high infant mortality rate. My favorite of the three editorials was titled "The Cheap Date:"

> Like a painted woman who expects the cheap evening she offers to attract potential dates, Alabama has for decades used its promise of low taxes to lure businesses and industry. It's about time this state learned what all cheap dates eventually discover: That they get taken advantage of.
>
> Too many businesses attracted by Alabama's low taxes have packed up and left after having a good time. Others remain but refuse to make the same commitment they make in other states. Even companies that do extensive business in Alabama won't put their headquarters here. Our low taxes aren't enough to provide the services and quality education they w a n t for their employees' and executives' families.
>
> Why are we so wedded to these low taxes that do us more harm than good? Because for decades our state government has not been in tune with the needs of the majority of our people. Even when it did try to act in our behalf, like a child who can't stand the taste of medicine, we often refused to acknowledge the benefits of a larger dose.
>
> Instead of doing the right thing, our lawmakers provide whatever taxes and services they can without disturbing ancient tax taboos. Then we try to put enough rouge and lipstick on the result to make it attractive.
>
> Our property tax system is a prime example. Alabama has, by far, the lowest property taxes in the nation. They got that way over a long, slow route along a path controlled by special interests.
>
> Alabama's 1901 constitution placed caps on the rate, but it did allow 100 percent of a property's appraised value to be taxed. That only stayed on the books until the Revenue Act of 1935 set a 60 percent assessment rate. But even that was not seriously collected. Alabama

CHAPTER 19

Power Co. eventually refused to pay it, saying non-utility taxpayers were "systematically and intentionally" assessed at only 40 percent.

Elected county tax assessors knew which side their bread was buttered on. The Alabama Supreme Court concurred and ordered Alabama Power's property tax assessment rate reduced to 40 percent. In 1967, L&N Railroad used the Alabama Power argument to have its rate reduced to 30 percent. The state then began assessing all utility and railroad property at 30 percent.

Later that year, lawmakers passed Act 502, which said that instead of 60 percent, the slice of a property's value to be taxed was "not to exceed 30 percent." That much latitude increased the inequities. The amount charged ranged from 8–28 percent, depending on the county.

A lawsuit filed in 1967 sought uniform assessments, saying the out-of-kilter system robbed schoolchildren in the lowest counties of the same chance for school funds the higher counties had. After a few rounds in litigation, in 1971 the court decided Act 502 was unconstitutional since it had originated in the Senate instead of the House, where revenue measures must begin.

In 1972, voters adopted the 325th amendment to the state constitution, which created three property tax classes. It lowered the assessment rate to 15 percent on most property. But it also formed a barrier to raising taxes on huge timber and agri-business tracts by placing them in the same category as private homes.

Shortly after, the Alabama Farm Bureau used the public's fear of high taxes on homeowners to campaign for passage of a "lid bill." The 1975 lid bill was supposed to limit to 20 percent the additional revenue a county could collect after reappraisals.

The Alabama Education Association, pointing out the lunacy in putting a lid on what were already the lowest property taxes in the nation, successfully fought the Farm Bureau proposal. But in 1978, Gov. George Wallace, threatening to expose certain legislators as tax hikers in an election year, steered a new "lid bill " through the Legislature.

Told by the Farm Bureau and timber companies that it would save homeowners tax dollars, voters approved it in a statewide referendum.

The Lid Law lowered the assessment ratio on most property

to 10 percent and set a cap on how much tax could be collected overall. It also made sure cities and counties would face one tough time raising property taxes. They had to call a public hearing, get permission from the Legislature, and then gain local voters' approval to do so.

Wallace's 1978 "Tax Relief Package" also installed a "current use" pro vision, which lets property owners have their land assessed without consideration of its real value, supposedly to protect the small farmer from taxes on higher land values caused by urban encroachment.

But it also cut in half taxes paid by huge timber, agribusinesses, and corporate landholders in its first year and shields their land against increases brought by re-evaluations today. The lid bill, current use: Sprinkle them with the various exemptions to the tax code and you can see why property taxes in Alabama are so low.

How low? According to the Advisory Commission on Intergovernmental Relations in Washington, in the U. S. in 1988 the average property tax paid per person was $538; in Florida, it was $537; in Georgia it was $396; in Tennessee it was $272; in Mississippi it was $266. In Alabama, it was $132.

That deprives our schools of local money because property taxes are the mainstay of local school support. Only 18.3 percent of our school revenue came from local levies last year. The national average was 43.7 percent.

Ridiculously low property taxes also tell large landholders to develop their lands elsewhere first; that they can afford to leave them alone here while the value increases, but taxes do not.

What incentives do we use to bring businesses into the state? We give them property tax breaks, of course. Industrial property tax exemptions are primarily the result of the Cater Act of 1949, authored by Sen. Silas D. Cater of Montgomery, and the Wallace Act of 1951, authored by a young state representative from Barbour County named George Wallace.

The Wallace-Cater Acts give cities and counties authority to set up industrial development boards that may exempt industries from local property taxes as a way to entice them to locate in the state.

Of course, these exemptions erode the tax base. And since they are for limited periods, they encourage industries to do business in Alabama only for as long as the exemptions are in effect.

CHAPTER 19

Allowed to raise their taxes to a level adequate to provide the quality of life all Americans covet; Alabamians would soon discover that this state doesn't have to be a cheap date to make others want to live and work here.

For too long, we have resembled one of those poor, backward Third World nations we ironically look at as beneath us.

Too often, others use our cheap labor to take our cheap natural resources, and then they sell the finished products back to us at a much higher price—as though we were some conquered colony.

If low property taxes are so good for us, why is it that despite paying by far the lowest taxes here of any state in the union, not one national timber company has located its headquarters in Alabama?

I learned after we won the Pulitzer that Ron had heard rumors of that possibility but never said anything to Joey or me. In fact, I was in the men's bathroom closest to the newsroom when the wire services began reporting Columbia University's 1991 Pulitzer recipients.

Two of my former health and science reporters, Bob Blalock and Jeff Hansen, barely gave me time to wash my hands before ushering me into the newsroom, where an impromptu celebration had already begun. Champagne showed up rather quickly, so someone must have anticipated the Pulitzer announcement, but I had no idea.

Making the event more special was receiving our Pulitzer certificates at Columbia University during its celebration of the seventy-fifth anniversary of the awards. All new and past Pulitzer recipients were invited. We were in awe rubbing shoulders with some of America's greatest writers, including Norman Mailer, Art Buchwald, and Arthur Schlesinger Jr. *New York Times* columnist Russell Baker, a two-time Pulitzer winner, was the keynote speaker. "It's a macabre experience to look out at this company and realize that I know how the obituaries of one half of you are going to begin," he quipped.

Also receiving Pulitzers that day were novelist John Updike for *Rabbit at Rest* and playwright Neil Simon for *Lost in Yonkers*, which Denice and I saw later that evening at a Broadway theater. After the play we met one of the play's featured actors, Bruno Kirby, whom we knew from movies like *City Slickers* and *The Godfather Part II*. We were eating dinner at nearby Sardi's restaurant when Kirby walked in. He was gracious enough to give Denice an autograph.

The next night we saw one of our favorite singers, Dianne Reeves, perform at the Blue Note Jazz Club.

As impressed as I was by the celebrities we saw, no one made more of an impression than the unassuming woman we met at the outdoor reception held after the Pulitzer ceremony at Columbia's Graduate School of Journalism. Looking for a place to sit amid the scattered tables, Denice and I spotted what looked like a good place to eat away from the crowd where only two people sat, a slightly built, bespectacled Black woman with gray hair and her younger companion.

Neither woman was eating. There was no food on their table. So, carefully clutching our small plates of finger food and beverages so as not to spill anything, we asked the women if we could join them. The younger woman smiled and said yes, while the older one merely smiled, so we sat down. I introduced myself and told them Denice was my wife. "I'm Nora Blakely," responded the younger woman, "and this is my mother, Gwendolyn Brooks."

I'm sure my jaw dropped. Simply by happenstance, we found ourselves sitting at the same picnic table at Columbia University with the first African American to win a Pulitzer Prize, Gwendolyn Brooks, who received her Pulitzer in 1950 for her book of poetry, *Annie Allen*.

The four of us made small talk; none of it memorable. In fact, Ms. Brooks said so little I don't remember any of her comments. Nora, meanwhile, put us at ease by asking questions about our young family. After forty-five minutes or so, we said we needed to go, and Nora gave me her card with a phone number and address in Chicago, where she said she could be reached if we were in the city. I never contacted her. Even with her invitation, I felt like that would be an intrusion that might mar the memories of a chance meeting I will forever treasure.

CHAPTER 20

LEAVING BIRMINGHAM AGAIN

Returning to the daily grind of writing editorials for the *News* didn't sit well after winning a Pulitzer Prize. Our lauded tax reform series generated much praise but little change in a state run by the same politicians and corporate barons who had for decades exploited the state's low-income and middle-class residents.

Also, although I was only thirty-eight, I felt as if I had already reached my ceiling for career advancement at the *News*. There seemed no likelihood of my ever succeeding Ron, who, at age forty, seemed similarly locked into his role as editorial page editor. Nor did I see me going back to the newsroom unless it was to take the same assistant city editor position that I had left to join the board.

My funky state of mind may have helped fuel an argument I got into with Ron when we were trying to do another editorial series, this one about Alabama's underfunded and failing public schools. I complained that the additional workload on top of our routine duties cranking out daily editorial and op-ed pages had become untenable. We shouted at each other and came close to calling each other names. But by lunch time we had gotten over it and went to eat with Joey at a nearby Chinese buffet.

The school funding series published in 1993 wound up becoming a Pulitzer Prize finalist, but the honor only made me want to leave the *News* even more. I wanted a job where the possibility of career advancement was more likely. I prayed about it and believed God answered me when a few months later I got a phone call from former *New York Times* senior editor Paul Delaney, a fellow Alabamian that I got to know at NABJ conventions.

A founding member of NABJ, Paul left the *Times* in 1992 to become chairman of the University of Alabama's journalism department. He asked me to become the Freedom Forum foundation's journalist-in-residence at the university. I didn't hesitate to say yes, knowing a paid sabbatical would give me time to figure out whether I really wanted to leave the *News*. I also thought it would be fun to return to the college campus where I decided as a high school freshman that I wanted to become a newspaperman.

The *News* approved my leave of absence, so twice a week, during the fall and spring semesters, I would commute sixty miles each way from Birmingham to Tuscaloosa to teach two classes. After a few weeks I regretted not living on campus so I could enjoy more daily interactions with my students. But with our children in middle school that would have placed a bigger burden on Denice, who had a job as well.

My workload also included participating in high school journalism workshops held across the state that were organized by the university-affiliated Alabama Scholastic Press Association (ASPA). Led by ASPA director Kathy Lawrence, our six-person team operated like a road show. We used a university van to travel to dozens of high school campuses within about one hundred miles of Tuscaloosa, where we provided hands-on instruction in reporting, headline writing, and newspaper page layout. It was fun and rewarding to maybe help those teenagers make a career choice.

Both Ed Mullins, the journalism school's dean, and Paul made sure I was treated like any other professor. So did the other professors, who would ask me to accompany them to lunch at their favorite Mexican restaurant. We ate burritos and tamales while they made jokes about the twists and turns involved in making a career in academia. I decided a similar quest for tenure wasn't what I wanted, though getting free faculty tickets to Alabama football games was an appealing incentive.

I was still on sabbatical from the *News* in 1994 when I got a call from Bill Marimow, managing editor of the *Baltimore Sun*, who I knew slightly from my short time at the *Inquirer*, when he won two Pulitzer Prizes for reporting. Denice and I attended one of the Pulitzer parties thrown in Bill's honor nearly a decade earlier at the Philadelphia Zoo. I was surprised when he telephoned me years later and offered me a job at the *Sun*. He said he wanted me to start

CHAPTER 20

work there as a reporter but that a higher position would be offered after I got to know Baltimore.

I hesitated at the thought of going back to reporting, but the *Sun* job would pay more than the *News*, and I took Bill's words as a guarantee that I would be promoted to a higher position. Denice and I discussed the pros and cons of leaving Birmingham, including our children not getting to go to high school with their friends. But in the end, we agreed that the opportunity being offered was too good to turn down. We also decided that with Mama no longer living in the projects since we had moved her into our old Birmingham house that she would be OK.

After an unsuccessful house-hunting trip to Baltimore, we decided to rent a home in Columbia, a leafy green "planned" suburb about twenty miles southwest of the city. Columbia banned billboards, restricted building heights, and had a town center in each of its ten "villages."

A year later, we bought a house in nearby Allview, which was in the same Howard County school district, so Dennis and Annette would not have to change schools like they did when they left friends behind in Birmingham. They seemed to thrive in Columbia. Annette was a cheerleader and played softball for Oakland Mills High School. Dennis was in the band, played baseball, and was on the Oakland Mills football team that won a state championship his senior year.

Mama turned eighty about three years after we moved to Maryland, and we again began worrying about her health. My brother Don had moved back to Birmingham and was teaching high school history, but told us he wanted to move back to the Pacific Northwest. Don didn't quickly establish roots after graduating from Eastern Washington University. Instead, he traveled the world serving in both the Coast Guard and the Army before becoming a teacher.

We didn't want Mama to be on her own if Don left Alabama, so we asked her to leave the house we still owned in Birmingham and move in with us in Maryland. Happy that she would get to live with her grandchildren, she said yes. So Don and I rented a U-Haul truck to move Mama's possessions, but we somehow failed to notice until it was time to hit the road that the seats in the small truck's cab couldn't be adjusted to accommodate Don's long legs. That meant I had to drive every one of the eight hundred miles to Maryland. Still, I enjoyed the long road trip as Don and I recalled old times and pondered the future.

Don had been married twice, and his past experience with being part of a military chain of command seemed to have made him more at ease with events as they happened. The brother I grew up with rarely backed down in any situation, but this Don seemed more willing to accept the reality that some situations, despite your best efforts, are simply beyond your control—like trying to drive a U-Haul truck whose cab is too tight for you to fit behind its steering wheel.

Meanwhile, at the *Sun*, I was trying to reestablish my footing as a general assignment reporter whose job was to answer the city editor's beck and call whenever and wherever there was a breaking story. A rare tornado that touched down in Baltimore on November 1, 1994, brought back memories of twister stories I wrote twenty years earlier in Alabama, but the different setting required a different lede.

"Harlem Park is one of those West Baltimore neighborhoods that is supposed to be without hope," I wrote. "The kind with crack dealers on street corners and old men drinking cheap wine on doorsteps. A neighborhood that would fall apart if disaster struck. That's what people who don't live in Harlem Park may think. But those who live there know better. When the tornadoes that touched down Tuesday left many in West Baltimore without food or shelter, they found hope in Harlem Park at Unity Methodist Church."

I interviewed Wyoming Carter, an eighty-year-old church member, as she stirred a pot of chicken and rice in the kitchen of the makeshift relief center. "We just try to do what needs to be done," she said.

Some assignments took me to neighborhoods that the paper's police reporter, David Simon, would later describe in his books *Homicide: A Year on the Killing Streets*, and *The Corner: A Year in the Life of an Inner-City Neighborhood*. It didn't take too long for me to learn that crack dealers didn't mind reporters so long as we didn't interfere with their commerce. Similarly, crack addicts avoided panhandling people who ask too many questions.

I didn't know Simon that well but sometimes ate lunch with a group of reporters that included him, Sandy Banisky, Rafael Alvarez, Michael Olesker, Mike Ollove, and Laura Lippman, whose father, Theo Lippman Jr., was a nationally syndicated columnist and on the *Sun*'s editorial board. Laura later married David, left journalism, and became a successful crime novelist.

We ate lunch either in the *Sun*'s cafeteria or at the Bridge, a nondescript diner located a short walk from the newspaper underneath a commuter bridge. The Bridge served large portions brought to tables tightly squeezed into its small dining room by waitresses who mostly managed not to bump into each

CHAPTER 20

other. I learned after a few visits to avoid sitting where you could see inside the greasy spoon's kitchen, because it looked like a bomb shelter. But the food was always hot and tasty.

With Marimow's recommendation, I found extra work as an adjunct professor of journalism at Loyola College of Maryland. Similarly to when I was a visiting professor at the University of Alabama, I taught an introductory journalism course and a senior seminar at Loyola. But journalism wasn't a major at the private Jesuit school, so my students either were taking the course out of curiosity or thought it would be easy. My best students had their sights on careers in law, medicine, or other sciences.

While juggling my Loyola and *Sun* jobs, I also contributed to a collection of essays edited by Gannett newspapers columnist DeWayne Wickham titled "Thinking Black." I knew DeWayne, a past president of the NABJ, from NABJ conventions. Other Black newspaper columnists with essays in DeWayne's book included Claude Lewis, *Philadelphia Inquirer*; Wiley Hall, *Baltimore Evening Sun*; Allegra Bennett, *Washington Times*; Richard Prince, *Rochester Democrat and Chronicle*; Derrick Z. Jackson, *Boston Globe*; Dwight Lewis, (Nashville) *Tennessean*, and Betty Baye, *Louisville Courier-Journal*.

Encouraged by DeWayne to write without the constraints typically placed on Black columnists by their publications, I decided to use a very atypical lede for my essay titled "A Message to Black Men":

> Pieces of dog were strewn across the highway. Some poor, dumb animal had exploded upon impact with a speeding vehicle. By the look of things, it probably was hit by one of those huge 18-wheelers.
>
> I kept driving, thinking about the dead animal, then about human lives taken prematurely: Martin Luther King Jr., Otis Redding, Arthur Ashe. My eyes stayed tuned to the road as my mind drifted in the opposite direction, to lives that seem inexhaustible. I thought of 101-year-old A. G. Gaston.

The essay argued that Gaston's story no longer inspired poor children who, like I had, were growing up in housing projects. For more than five decades until his death in 1996, the former coal miner was the richest Black man in Alabama and one of the richest in America. He owned a bank, insurance company, funeral home, radio station, and construction business, but even before he died, his name had become meaningless to Black children.

"They cannot make the connection between his economic struggle and their desperately poor lives," I said, recalling a 1992 interview I did with Gaston for *Black Enterprise* magazine. The millionaire said he knew he was called an Uncle Tom for seeming too willing to appease Birmingham's white business establishment, but he said he had no regrets. "I was the only nigger in the group, you know, and had money, too. I got opportunity because of that. I got the franchise for the radio station. I never would have gotten it if I hadn't been a good nigger."

I didn't respond to Gaston's words, knowing I needed to complete my interview. But the militancy I espoused twenty years earlier as a college student was screaming in my ear. I stopped myself from disagreeing with him by reminding myself that Gaston had quietly helped fund Birmingham's civil rights movement, put up the money to bail Martin Luther King Jr. out of jail, and negotiate the deal to integrate department stores that ended the marches and boycott. "If I hadn't been an Uncle Tom, there wouldn't be what we have today," Gaston told me.

I wanted the essay to make the point that Black men who continue to be disproportionately unemployed, imprisoned, and likely to die young, need not become "good niggers," as Gaston put it. But, I said in the essay, they "must have the strength, the courage, the desire to adapt to this changing world, bending and flexing, and—by any means necessary—making the moves it takes to progress, to go forward, to reach the day when racism cannot exist because skin color is no longer a condition of power."

Writing for Dewayne's book provided some respite from my frustration with still being a general assignment reporter for the *Sun*. But one day when I felt I couldn't take it anymore, I asked Marimow for a meeting and told him I no longer had the legs or enthusiasm to hit the streets looking for a story. He said he understood and after another Black reporter, Mike Fletcher, decided to leave the *Sun* to work for the *Washington Post*, Bill assigned me to take his place working with city hall reporters Eric Siegel and JoAnna Daemmrich.

I had covered Birmingham's first Black mayor, Richard Arrington Jr., for UPI in the 1980s, so I looked forward to covering Baltimore's first Black mayor, Kurt Schmoke. I also wondered, though, if Bill's giving me a city hall job meant I was no longer being considered for the higher-level position he had dangled as an enticement to get me to come to Baltimore. Bill had won two Pulitzer Prizes for investigative reporting, which wasn't my strength. Maybe he had decided I wasn't what he wanted in a newsroom editor.

CHAPTER 20

Not long after I began covering city hall, Bill replaced the *Sun*'s Black city editor, Mike Adams, with Jim Asher. Like me, Jim had worked with Bill years earlier at the *Inquirer*. I didn't know Jim, but our relationship seemed fine until the day I questioned the priority of an assignment his assistant city editor deputy asked me to cover. It was some puff piece involving an event at the Enoch Pratt public library, and I was already working on what I thought was a more important story.

The deputy told Asher I was complaining. He immediately came to my desk, and we got into a somewhat heated discussion that ended abruptly when he told me, "You've been trouble ever since you got here." Since Asher hadn't been at the *Sun* "ever since" I got there, I wondered how he came to that conclusion. Who had he been talking to? Regardless, not wanting to be anyone's "trouble," I again asked Marimow for an audience and asked him to help me get on the *Sun*'s editorial board.

Bill didn't seem surprised, so maybe after talking to Asher, he, too, realized my return to reporting after not doing it for a decade wasn't working out. Still, he suggested I might regret leaving the newsroom. As Bill spoke slowly and softly, I felt as if I were listening to Don Corleone as portrayed by Marlon Brando in *The Godfather*. "You know, I won't be able to help you if you leave the newsroom," Bill said.

Not wanting to sound ungrateful, I said, "I know," the entire time thinking, "I'll be fine if you open the door for me." We chatted a bit more before he agreed to talk to the *Sun*'s editorial page editor, Joseph R. L. Sterne. Bill cautioned that was no guarantee of a transfer, but within a few weeks I was writing editorials for the *Sun* and its sister publication, the *Evening Sun*.

Sterne assigned me to cover city government with another editorial writer, Antero Pietila, a native Finn who had lived in the United States since 1964. Antero's charming wife, Barbara, was a Black artist who sewed intricate quilts similar to the mosaics depicting Black culture sewn by the world-famous quilters in Gee's Bend, Alabama. I was well familiar with their work and was amazed by Barbara's. She and Antero treated Denice and me like old friends. I was enjoying my work, enjoying living in Columbia, enjoying that our kids were doing well in high school, enjoying life. Then came that telephone call from San Francisco. "Calvin doesn't know I'm calling, but there's something you need to know. Calvin is sick. He's dying. Of AIDS."

CHAPTER 21

NEVER ASKED CALVIN IF HE WAS GAY

My youngest brother, Calvin, moved to San Francisco after he graduated from the University of Iowa, but even though he was thousands of miles away, we tried to maintain some of the closeness we had as children.

Sometimes Denice and I were in Birmingham when he would come home for Christmas, but he also visited us in Maryland when I was working for the *Baltimore Sun*. That happened in 1995, two years before Mama left Alabama to live with my family of four in Columbia, Maryland, when both she and Calvin traveled to our home for the Christmas holidays.

I took it for granted that Calvin was gay by then, but never brought it up. Neither did he. We preferred spending most of our time together rehashing childhood memories. But I noticed Calvin seemed more pensive that Christmas. He blamed his mood on a sore toe, so I left it at that, not wanting anything to spoil our time with Mama. She was seventy-nine years old, and we didn't know how many more Christmases we would have with her.

Calvin was supposed to sleep on the sofa-bed in our basement family room, but after he had difficulty sleeping, he and my 14-year-old son Dennis traded bedrooms. Otherwise, everyone ate a lot, talked a lot, laughed a lot, and generally enjoyed each other's company.

A few days after Calvin returned to San Francisco, we got a letter from him reiterating just how much fun it had been for him to be with us. I didn't detect it then, but rereading that letter after Calvin's death, I detected what

CHAPTER 21

seemed like subtle hints that he thought that Christmas might be his last. This is what he wrote:

> Hello, you two. I hope this finds the Jacksons of Baltimore all healthy and happy. I'm OK. I can't believe how long it is taking this in-grown toenail to heal. I'm not scheduled to see the podiatrist again until next month (re my curling toes). Trust it will be totally better by then.
>
> I'm sending D. J. this sweatshirt to show my appreciation for his letting me have his bedroom while there. I must admit I slept much more comfortably in his room than I did in the basement room, or do you call it Family Room II, and Family Room I is upstairs by the kitchen (smiley face).
>
> Boy! Am I glad that Mama and I made it back to our homes before the blizzard hit you there. But I suppose a snowstorm wouldn't have bothered us too much so long as I had plenty to eat. I've got to learn how to make ox-tail soup. Yum.
>
> I can't thank you both enough for giving me such a wonderful Christmas. I enjoyed every minute being there. Just letting me be there is all the gifts I'll ever need from you. I think Mama enjoyed herself too.
>
> You know now if you didn't already know that I truly love strolling down memory lane. I surprise myself with how good my memory is (Julia Mae-hey-hey!).
>
> I meant to ask Annette Michelle if she still remembers the "Thumbelina" song I taught her when she was just a little girl. I'm so glad that I got to teach them the "Praise Him" song. Truth be told, I made up that little song myself and sing it for inspiration.
>
> Peter and I went to see Oliver Stone's *Nixon*. Three long hours. I think it was good because they focused so much on Pat. That poor woman. Never envy a first lady.
>
> I could write more but it's getting late, and I know my penmanship is reflecting that. Imagine what it would look like if I didn't have paper with lines.

The letter abruptly ends there, without so much as a "Yours truly," and I can't help but think that either his pain or his medication prevented Calvin from writing another word.

NEVER ASKED CALVIN IF HE WAS GAY

I didn't really think much about Calvin over the next five months. Denice and I returned to our routine of work and raising two teenagers, never thinking we would soon be experiencing one tragedy that would reveal a second.

On May 12, 1996, my oldest brother, Anthony, unexpectedly died. "Skippy" had suffered grand mal seizures ever since his car was hit by a tractor-trailer truck on Interstate 59, just south of Tuscaloosa, on May 16, 1982. A violent seizure fourteen years later left Skippy dead four months before his fiftieth birthday. He left behind his wife, Ollie Jean, and three young sons, Chris, Greg, and Brian.

Mama never remarried, so Skippy had been the "man" of our family ever since Daddy died in 1967. He became the adult role model we younger brothers looked to when seeking wisdom on any subject involving growing up. Skip had a contagious smile and the gift of effortless conversation that helped him turn casual acquaintances into lifelong friends. I wasn't surprised when a few years before his death Skip got the call to preach and began studying to become a minister.

As shocking as Skippy's death was, I was almost as upset when Calvin told me he wouldn't be coming home for the funeral. Don had returned to Birmingham to live, and Jeffery and his family were flying in from Oregon. I couldn't envision Calvin not being with his brothers and Mama. He said he had a bad tooth that made it too painful for him to travel, but I didn't buy it.

"No excuse is good enough to miss your big brother's funeral," I thought. But I wasn't about to argue. I had lost one brother to death. I didn't need to lose another due to hard feelings. I knew Calvin had a better excuse for not coming home but wasn't ready to reveal it.

So we buried Skippy in a little cemetery not far from where his family lived in Greene County, Alabama. As we drove the eighty-five miles from Birmingham to get there, I couldn't help returning again and again in my mind to Calvin's lame excuse that he had a toothache.

It was four months later that I learned the truth. That's when Calvin's friend Ricky Marquis called me from San Francisco while I was sitting at my desk at the *Baltimore Sun* to tell me my little brother was in the final stages of dying from AIDS.

CHAPTER 22

LOVE IS MEDICINE

When I got home from work, I called Calvin, who apparently was sleeping or didn't want to talk to me. His roommate, Peter, picked up the phone, which in itself was confirmation of their true relationship. He and Calvin had shared an apartment for several years, but I knew little about Peter other than the fact that he was white.

Peter said neither he nor Calvin knew Ricky was going to call me but that he was relieved to no longer be an accomplice to Calvin's keeping a secret from his family. I said I wanted to come to San Francisco, and Peter said I should but that didn't need to happen immediately. A few days later I got a letter from Peter that detailed what he had done for my brother. I think sharing that letter is the best way to let Peter tell his story, so here it is:

> Dear Harold,
>   I am sorry that you had to receive the news about Calvin the way you did. On the other hand, I am very happy that you know. It was nice to finally speak to you on the telephone, and I hope one day to meet you and maybe your family.
>   As you know, Calvin and I have lived together for about four years. Before I got seriously involved with him, he informed me that he was HIV-positive, which I am sure was not an easy thing to do. I am HIV-negative myself and have remained so to this date. I gather

from what he has told me that he first became aware of his HIV status in the late '80s.

The first two years were relatively uneventful, with respect to his disease. In 1994, he developed pneumonia in April and again in June, which was treated. It was diagnosed as walking pneumonia. In July he started complaining about back pains, but his doctor back then dismissed it as a sprained muscle. In late September, the pains become so unbearable one weekend that when he finally made it to the doctor the following Monday and they ran a bunch of tests, it turned out to be a pulmonary embolism (blood clot) in his lungs and he was hospitalized immediately.

The situation then was grave indeed, but he recovered. Although in my opinion, he never regained his strength after that incident. For the next six months, he increasingly complained about being tired and falling asleep at work. Quite frankly, I don't know how he lasted as long at his job as he did, but he did have a low-pressure position.

In April 1995, we started looking into the ramifications of long-term/permanent disability and he stopped working on the last day of June. Throughout September he received state disability and full pay from his job. From October till January, he only received state disability, but his employer paid for his health insurance. In January, Social Security disability started up and his long-term disability started as well. Presently, his state disability is exhausted, but he gets Social Security disability together with his long-term disability pay.

In July 1995, we moved to a two-bedroom apartment in Oakland. In hindsight, that was not a good move as this location was away from friends and had less public transport than Calvin was used to. He always called that location "Bosnia/Herzegovina." It was a nice apartment but away from things and friends.

My work required that I drive all over, but he increasingly got frustrated with being left alone and told me to stop working, which I did not do at that time. He started on a drug trial with the protease inhibitor Saquinavir around late August and also started having trouble with his bowel movements.

During our trip to New York in November he had several near accidents, which caused grief and embarrassment. You indicated that

CHAPTER 22

you noticed that things were not quite OK when he visited you for Christmas. Now you know.

We went on another trip to New York in late February and this time we made sure to minimize all walking by taking taxis. But in all honesty, Calvin spent most of the time there in the hotel room and I had to bring food to the room. We managed to see two shows and had half a restaurant meal. In the airports, he got wheelchair assistance, which was a blessing.

In March, he developed pneumonia once again, which was treated by his doctor who prescribed infusions that I administered over the course of one week after having been instructed by a nurse. We started to realize that we better move back to San Francisco because his hospital and doctor were both there. From March on, Calvin started walking even less, so he got a walker and then a bedside commode as getting from the bedroom to the bathroom became an increasingly difficult task. We also got a wheelchair at that time.

In May, we started getting health aides to come to the house a few days a week. By the time we moved, Calvin was for all intents and purposes completely unable to walk. The move to our apartment in San Francisco was done with the help of professional movers. Calvin spent the day at a friend's place with a health aide.

While our new apartment is a bit smaller, it is still reasonably big, and the other great thing is that we are allowed to have a dog. We had previously tried to get permission to have a dog, but our landlords refused. So, the day after the move a friend came over and sat with Calvin while I drove to Sacramento and picked up a Lhasa Apso puppy, "Barkley." I have been determined that Calvin experience having a dog.

Since that time, his legs have become even less functional although he has feeling in them. He had a bout with thrush (Candida), which had to be treated with a week of Amphotericin infusions followed by a week of antibiotics. Throughout all this time his appetite has been good, and he is in a relatively pain-free situation, with the exception of joint pain from lying in bed all the time.

He has also become increasingly confused and disoriented, to the point that he may ask what day it is and not remember the answer five minutes later. Keeping track of morning and night has also become an issue of concern. As I mentioned, I have stopped working completely so that I can be with him as much as possible.

He is now receiving hospice care at home, which means a health aide comes in every day for about six hours and helps get him cleaned up, fed, and does some light housekeeping, cooking, etc., which also gives me a chance to get out. He receives in-home visits from a nurse twice a week and we also get a physical therapist and a massage therapist once a week.

In general, Calvin does not care for the thought of me leaving the apartment even when somebody is with him. I am screening most telephone calls and he typically does not want to see or talk to anyone as it tires him out.

Calvin has not been very good at taking the medicine prescribed, and as you know you cannot force medicine down a patient's throat. Once you have spoken with Calvin again, I cannot see any reason why you could not speak to his doctor. Although I have not asked for a time frame from her, she has indicated to me that I am probably the reason he is still here. She has told me that he has a strong heart, and as I mentioned previously his appetite is still reasonably good.

I have long been an advocate of Calvin telling you what is going on. But whenever I raise the issue, Calvin has always rejected it outright, saying it would give Janye a heart attack. His doctor did talk to Calvin last week and suggested that now was probably a good time to notify the family and that she would be happy to volunteer if he so desired. Calvin was all smiles until she left, at which point he got very angry and told me she had overstepped her bounds and who did she think she is.

Well, I have not been forcing the issue since I am the one living here. But Rick Marquis took things in his own hands and contacted you, and I am happy that I don't have to be a guardian of this family secret any longer. I realize that you now have to agonize with this situation, but in the long run it is better that it happen now rather than after the fact.

I have entertained the thought of Janye coming to see him (as well as yourself). I'm not sure how she would be able to handle it, but in my experience, mothers are very strong and capable of a lot in situations like this. Give it some thought (as will I) and let me know what you want to do.

CHAPTER 22

As I indicated on the telephone, I would prefer that you keep what you know to yourself when you talk to Calvin. I have tried to provide you with some details in this letter, so that you may better understand what is going on.

At this point, you may assure Janye that Calvin is as comfortable as can be expected, in his own home, around his own things. This is important, as opposed to being in a nursing home, which was an option we thought about (and rejected) about one month ago. It may be an option again if his situation worsens. In any event, I want to keep him at home for as long as possible.

CHAPTER 23

THE SECRETS WE KEEP

Peter's letter didn't prepare me for how frail Calvin looked when I got to San Francisco about two weeks later. Seeing my little brother in their small apartment, propped up with pillows in a hospital bed, I thanked God that he moved to California after college. I don't think an AIDS patient in the 1990s would have received the same elevated level of care in Alabama.

I was only going to be in San Francisco a few days, but Calvin insisted that Peter show me some of its fabled tourist sites—the Golden Gate Bridge, the Presidio, Fisherman's Wharf, and their favorite barbecue joint. No doubt Peter would have preferred to stay by Calvin's bedside, but he tried to fulfill all my dying brother's requests. Even without the legal status of a spouse, Peter had maneuvered through California's health-care system to get Calvin every benefit he qualified for.

I should have spent more time getting to know Peter. Instead, Calvin and I fell into our old habit of revisiting old memories. We both knew he was dying, but neither of us wanted to talk about that. So we didn't. When it finally came time to return home, I told Calvin I loved him, hugged him in his bed, and headed out the door to prepare for my flight back to Baltimore. Just like at Daddy's funeral, I didn't cry. The Jackson boys aren't supposed to do that.

Two months later, I got the telephone call from Peter telling me Calvin had died. I began 1996 with four brothers, never thinking for a second that I would end it with two. I wrote about Calvin's death in a column published a

CHAPTER 23

week later in the *Baltimore Sun*. Headlined "The Secrets That We Keep," it began with a description of how I received the news:

> Awake at 2:30 last Saturday night, I was struck by how well I could see across the length and breadth of my bedroom. A flood of moonlight filtered through the blinds, giving every object a shadowy dimension that suggested an attachment to another world.
>
> I put on my glasses, walked barefoot across the cool, hardwood floor and peeked out the window. The sky was actually cloudy save for an occasional break, the largest of which allowed the moon to fully display the illuminating power that according to legend can drive men mad.
>
> The sun would blind us if we similarly looked directly at it. But the moon, in its brilliantly pale fluorescence, demands that we stare it in the face. I opened the blinds wider to get a better look at the glowing disc with dark craters that make it a work of art.
>
> Eventually, though, without slippers or robe, I started to get cold. And was reluctantly reminded of what woke me up in the first place. A call informing me that my younger brother had died.

Calvin's story wasn't unique. An estimated nine hundred thousand people in the United States were HIV-positive when he died in 1996. More than thirty-one thousand of those patients died that year, which was 50 percent less than the year before. That's thanks to previously unavailable antiviral drug therapies. Many who died didn't know they were sick until it was too late. Others kept their diagnosis to themselves, hoping for a miracle cure.

There's still no cure for AIDS, but drug therapies still in their development stage when Calvin died are keeping people alive now by dramatically reducing the amount of virus in their blood. Such drugs not only are more affordable; they are also being sold by pharmaceutical companies in TV ads featuring obviously gay couples.

So much has changed. I can't help thinking that were Calvin still alive, he would be healthier and happier. He no longer would feel the need to keep his truth a secret.

CHAPTER 24

LIVING IN FEAR OF BEING FIRED

Calvin's death was followed by one of the most trying experiences I'd had as a journalist. Joe Sterne retired in 1997 after twenty-five years as the *Baltimore Sun*'s editorial page editor, and even though I thought his longtime deputy, Barry Rascovar, would get the job, I applied for it too. I'm sure Barry was as surprised as I was when the *Sun*'s new publisher, Mary E. Junck, instead hired Jacqueline Thomas, a Black woman who had been the *Detroit News*'s Washington bureau chief.

I told some other editorial board members that I felt my chances to replace Joe would have been greater had he backed me instead of Barry, who in my mind represented the past, not the future. Word of my complaint somehow got to Joe, who felt so strongly about my perceived slight that he wrote me a letter dated April 15, 1997.

"Just to clarify the record," it said, "I want you to know that I was in no way 'reluctant' to have you join our editorial staff. On the contrary, I was quite glad you made the switch to the fourth floor—and never once did I regret your move. You have been a fine colleague. . . . Perhaps I was not the 'advocate' for your candidacy that you wanted me to be, but that was because of my loyalty to another one of my colleagues. I think you can understand that. I wish you all the best in your career. I always have. And I hope you regard me as a friend—as I do you."

I assured Jackie after her arrival that despite having competed for the job

CHAPTER 24

she now held, as a fellow African American I wanted her to succeed. My good wishes apparently fell on deaf ears. Naively, I believed Jackie would no longer consider me a competitor, but her actions soon proved me wrong. Only a few months passed before she reassigned me from covering Baltimore city government to writing editorials about Howard County from the *Sun*'s suburban news bureau in Columbia.

The bureau was only ten minutes from my house, meaning I no longer had to commute nineteen miles each way to the *Sun* building in downtown Baltimore. That meant I could attend some of the baseball and softball games my son and daughter played at their high school. But I wanted to cover city hall. I had good sources there and a list of editorials I wanted to write. Jackie's transfer felt like an unfair demotion, and as our relationship got worse, I feared she was trying to find a way to fire me.

My suspicions seemed validated when one day, out of the blue, she accused me of insubordination. Jackie said I had refused to write an editorial assigned to me by Carol Stevens, who replaced Rascovar, who quit after Jackie arrived, as assistant editorial page editor. I told Jackie that Carol never did more than smile when I said I would write the editorial when I returned from a scheduled vacation. But when Jackie stuck to her insubordination accusation, it was clear she wanted me gone.

I prayed that I would have time to leave on my terms, and God heard me. I was still writing editorials and a weekly column from Howard County when I got a telephone call in 1999 from the *Philadelphia Inquirer*'s South Jersey editor, Julie Busby. In its latest push to boost revenue by increasing suburban readership, the *Inquirer* wanted to create a daily commentary page in the newspaper's local news section for readers on the other side of the Delaware River in South Jersey.

Julie asked me if I wanted to be the commentary page's editor, and I jumped at the chance to leave the *Sun* before Jackie fired me. Call it coincidence, but the *Sun*'s other two Black editorial board members, Marilyn McCraven and Norris West, also left the paper after Jackie became editorial page editor.

I was happy to be back at the *Inquirer* after a thirteen-year absence, even if it wasn't as an editorial board member. Instead, I worked under Julie in the South Jersey newsroom. I designed the commentary page to look like an editorial page. It even had daily cartoons drawn by freelancers. There were letters to the editor, but no staff-written editorials, and guest columns provided by more than sixty freelance writers that I recruited, most of them women. Some had journalism backgrounds, but most were homemakers or had other jobs but had always wanted to be published writers.

The commentary page provided a forum for South Jersey residents to discuss what they felt was important outside Philadelphia. They wrote about politics, education, crime, religion, child rearing, growing old, and grief. My most frequent contributor was Sally Friedman, the wife of a retired judge whose columns included one that resonated with me as a father about how difficult it was for her to cede the responsibility of hosting Passover seders to her adult daughters.

The South Jersey page was a success, and in 2002 the *Inquirer* decided to publish a commentary page for readers inside the city limits and one for readers in Philadelphia's Pennsylvania suburbs. My operation was then transferred to the editorial board, and I was given the title of coordinator to supervise production of all three commentary pages and a Sunday "Voices" section featuring readers opinions in various formats.

Two years later, I was promoted to assistant editorial page editor, and in 2007 I became editorial page editor when Chris Satullo resigned to become the *Inquirer*'s director of civic engagement. Chris had created that job, which grew out of the board's collaboration with the University of Pennsylvania and other organizations to create jointly held public forums and other events aimed at improving life in Philadelphia.

CHAPTER 25

FILLING THE GAPS IN MAMA'S STORY

Mama died on September 7, 2009, almost two years after I was named the *Inquirer*'s editorial page editor and just three days after Jayla, the first of our three grandchildren, was born. Her sister, Alaina, was born in 2013, and their cousin Maddox, seven years later.

Some of my first thoughts after Mama died were of all the things I should have asked her but never did. "What a lousy reporter I've been when it comes to my own family," I thought. Genealogical research after Mama's death has filled in some gaps, but I still don't know things that she either kept secret, didn't know, or didn't care to discuss.

I do know that Janye Lee Wilson was born January 22, 1916, in a little Pike County, Alabama, town called Troy. Her mother was Lula Mae Jones and her father was Ace Wilson. Mama never knew her daddy. She said kinfolks told her a white man put a "walking spell" on Ace soon after her birth and he disappeared. The truth, however, may be a different story.

Census records for Troy in the year Janye was born show only one "Ace" Wilson among the town's four thousand residents, and he was a white man. That Ace was the son of Lizzie and Samuel P. Wilson, a local farmer who was the grandson of Mary and James M. Wilson, who fought for the Confederacy as a private in the Forty-Sixth Alabama Infantry. Ace was twenty-two when Janye was born, and Lula was eighteen. In such a small town, did Janye's and

Ace's paths ever cross? Did they have a secret relationship that led to Mama's birth? I'll likely never know.

Soon after Janye's birth, her mother, Lula, grandmother Sara Jane, and Sara Jane's husband, Lonzo Dubose, left Troy and moved 140 miles away to Birmingham. Lonzo had been a tenant farmer who paid rent to the man who owned the land he farmed. It's likely he left Troy after growing tired of laboring long and hard for little return. But maybe he left because his stepdaughter said Ace Wilson was her child's father and insisted on giving the baby Ace's surname, Wilson. If Mama ever learned the truth, she never revealed it to her children.

Lonzo found an ironworks job in Birmingham to provide for his bustling household, which included not only his wife, Sara Jane; stepdaughter, Lula; and her baby, Janye, but also a son, Verland, and three daughters: Hannah, Myrtis, and Gladis. But three years after Janye's birth, Lula died. She was only twenty-one and the circumstances were not recorded, but I suspect she was a Spanish flu victim. More than fifteen thousand flu victims died in Alabama during the 1918–19 pandemic. Janye grew up calling Sara Jane and Lonzo "Mama" and "Poppa."

Two younger cousins, Carey Bean and William Whiteside, later joined the Dubose household. Mama and the two boys became playmates, but she said she also had daily chores to perform, including feeding the chickens and making coffee every morning for the adults. After three years at Parker High School, Mama took classes at a local "beauty college" and briefly worked in her friend Marie King's hairdresser shop. She became a movie theater cashier but eventually joined the throng of Black women riding the bus over Red Mountain to cook and clean for white families in Birmingham's suburbs.

I never told Mama, but the culinary skills she honed cooking for white folks put money in my pocket when I was in elementary school. She always put a slice of cake in her boys' sack lunches, and I would sell mine for ten cents. Those dimes bought me ice cream in the school cafeteria or store candy on the way home. Mama deserved a share of my profits, but I didn't dare tell her what I was doing. It would have hurt her pride to know one of her children was selling pieces of cake to his more affluent schoolmates to earn dimes.

There was never a weekend when Mama wasn't baking either a cake, a pie, or cookies. She even made pecan pralines and coconut macaroons. Christmas meant buying pounds of nuts and candied fruit to bake the fruit cakes that became our family's gifts. Pound cake, however, was Mama's specialty, so much so

CHAPTER 25

that when her baking skills declined as she reached her eighties, Mama would throw pound cakes that didn't meet her standards into the garbage can and start over. Mama believed in the adage "waste not, want not," but it didn't apply to substandard pound cakes. It didn't matter that they tasted good; they also had to look as if they had been perfectly baked.

Mama wasn't just a good baker. Almost everything she cooked was delicious, especially chicken, which we ate fried, roasted, barbecued, stewed with potatoes and carrots, or simmered in broth with dumplings. Like most Black families that we knew, we also ate almost anything pork, from brains scrambled with eggs for breakfast, to neck bones, pig tails, pig feet, and yes, chitlins for dinner. Mama warned us, though, to never trust anyone to clean chitlins as carefully as she did.

The only time I had trouble swallowing something Mama cooked was when she served a couple of rabbits that an old hunting buddy of Daddy's had brought us. The hunter purportedly used a bull whip to put down his small prey. The story didn't discourage me, but I lost my appetite after watching Daddy skin and gut the rabbits in our apartment's small utility room near the back door. Mama seasoned, floured, and fried the rabbits to a golden brown like chicken, and they looked delicious, but unable to get the sight of Daddy eviscerating the dead bunnies out of my head, I couldn't eat my meal.

Mama was just as good cooking the fresh vegetables usually found on Southern tables, from black eyed peas that we shelled, string beans that we snapped, and corn that we shucked to collard greens, turnip greens, mustard greens, butter beans, beets, okra, tomatoes, and Irish or sweet potatoes. Most of our produce was purchased from our tall, burly "vegetable man," Mr. Cecil, who, with his only arm, traversed neighborhoods in an old, squeaking bus whose seats had been replaced by crates filled with vegetables, fruits, and sometimes fresh fish on ice.

More importantly, Mr. Cecil sold candy and cookies, most of it for a penny or two and nothing for more than a nickel, which made his bus a happy place for children. We would gleefully climb aboard his mobile treat shop and beg our mamas to add some Apple Stix, Mary Janes, root beer barrels, oatmeal raisin cookies, or, my favorite, Stage Planks molasses cookies to their purchases. If not that, then maybe some sugar cane, which we ate like it was candy.

Mama at some point moved out of her grandparents' house and lived with her aunt Hannah, whose husband, Lee Thomas, shoveled coal into train engine boilers as a steam locomotive fireman. The Thomases' son, Mullie, and daughter, Mary, also lived in their big house in the Titusville community, less than a mile from the Loveman Village projects, where I grew up, would later be built. I remember my brothers and me sitting on Auntie and Uncle's front porch swing snacking on figs and pecans from trees in their backyard.

Mama was likely living with Auntie and Uncle when she started dating Lorenzo Whitehead, a handsome man whose photo I found one day as a teenager while rambling through Mama's old cedar chest. They were married in 1940, but whatever love they had didn't last. Mama said she left Whitehead the first time he hit her. I don't know how much time passed between that incident and their divorce in 1945. Later that same year, Mama married Daddy, Lewis Jackson.

How did Janye meet Lewis? I don't know. Growing up I never thought of them as ever being anything but a couple. When I finally thought to question Mama about such matters, she was in her eighties and either didn't want to discuss details or didn't remember them. She suggested her memory was so cluttered with information accumulated over nearly nine decades that she had forgotten some details. I'm still ashamed that as someone who prided himself on being a good reporter, I failed to get my own mother's whole story.

Daddy died when I was fourteen years old, so I'm somewhat justified in having never interrogated him, but I was fifty-six when Mama died and never properly interviewed her. Even so, I don't think I would have learned anything to change my belief that Mama and Daddy were the only parents I could ever want.

Daddy's premature death at age fifty-eight didn't deprive me or my four brothers of the types of lessons any son would want from his father. Daddy and Mama taught us to be men who could be counted on in good times, and bad. They taught us to work hard whether we're mopping floors or building empires and to never go looking for trouble.

Mama and Daddy rarely embraced romantically around their boys, but I never doubted their love for each other. They hardly ever argued in our presence, and when they did, it was brief and concluded without any noticeably lingering animosity. Like many couples, Mama and Daddy seemed to have a symbiotic relationship, with each one conveying thoughts and feelings to the other without saying a word. Together they were the powerful team whose stable marriage was our family's glue.

Eerily, just like when Calvin died thirteen years earlier, I received word of Mama's death via a late Monday night phone call. And just as it was with

CHAPTER 25

Calvin's death, it wasn't a surprise. Mama was ninety-three and had seemed to get weaker each successive year after suffering a stroke when she was eighty-one and living with us in Maryland. We moved to New Jersey in 1999, and about two years later, as Mama's health continued to decline, Denice and I began discussing whether to move her into a nursing home.

I kept thinking about Mama's decision to move Daddy into a nursing home in Alabama, only to see him die there within a few weeks. But with our children away at college and Denice and me both working, we decided Mama needed more than a home health aide to assist her when we weren't home. Kresson View was larger than we wanted but that was an asset in that it provided twenty-four-hour medical care, physical therapy, and group activities to help maintain its residents' mental health. Even so, every time I visited Mama, I felt guilty that I wasn't bringing her home.

It was about two o'clock in the morning when I got the call telling me Mama had died. I told Denice, who also had been awakened by the phone's ring. I got dressed and drove to the nursing home in a neighboring town, Voorhees, New Jersey. I don't remember turning on the car radio. If I did, I didn't hear whatever music was playing. I was trying to mentally prepare myself for what I would soon see.

After arriving, I took the elevator to Mama's floor, where a nurse expressed her sorrow before taking me to the still, dimly lit room. Mama was lying in her bed, its covers drawn up to her neck. I could hear the soft snoring of her roommate, who slept obliviously on the other side of the hospital curtain that divided their room. I don't know if she was awake when the staff discovered Mama had died.

Mama looked like she was sleeping too. I was thankful for that. It allowed me to believe she had died peacefully, perhaps dreaming about her childhood, or Daddy, or what cake she should bake for her boys—coconut or caramel? Mama had worked and prayed so hard for her family for so many years. Worn out now, she deserved to rest. Briefly, I held her cold hand and cried.

We flew Mama back to Birmingham for her funeral at Westminster Presbyterian Church. My brothers Jefferey and Don were there. So were my son, Dennis; daughter, Annette; her husband, Harvey Wolff; and their baby girl, Jayla, who was born three days before Mama died. I thank God that I got to show Mama a photo of Jayla the day before she died. When Mama smiled, I remembered her once telling me that she had always wanted a daughter.

Now she had a great-granddaughter, Jayla, and two granddaughters, Annette and Maiya, Jeffery's little girl.

The closeness of Mama's death to Jayla's birth makes me think that seeing that photo of her great-grandchild gave her the peace of mind to rest her tired body. Mama did so much for her family, but most importantly, she prayed for our safekeeping. Perhaps after seeing a photo of her great-granddaughter, she felt it was OK to pass the reins.

Jeff, Don, and I gave eulogies at the funeral, but I have no recollection of what either of us said. We didn't cry. A short procession of six or seven cars followed Mama's hearse about two miles to Grace Hill Cemetery, a Black graveyard only a few blocks from traditionally white Elmwood Cemetery, which is where legendary University of Alabama football coach Bear Bryant and other white luminaries are buried.

I don't know if any Black luminaries are buried in Grace Hill, but the two most important people in my life are there—buried less than two miles from where they raised five boys in the Loveman Village housing project.

Mama was buried next to Daddy on one of the cemetery's small hills. A double headstone that already included Daddy's name, birth date, and death date was already on the site. All we needed to do was add Mama's death date to her side of the stone. Standing and watching as her casket was being lowered into the grave, I found comfort in my Christian belief that I will see her again. Daddy, Skippy, and Calvin too.

Maybe in heaven we will laugh about the good times, and bad, we had while living under God's sun. Maybe we'll fill in some of the gaps in our stories that we left unfinished when we were alive. Maybe we will admit that keeping secrets is more likely to weaken a family's bond than strengthen it. The Roman poet Virgil centuries ago said, "Love conquers all." But that's harder when secrets standing in love's way aren't told.

CHAPTER 26

AVOIDING THE NOOSE-STRANGLING NEWSPAPERS

Not long after Mama's death, I found myself struggling to survive the financial tailspin that almost killed my employer, the *Philadelphia Inquirer*. It, the *Philadelphia Daily News*, and thirty-one other newspapers owned by the Knight Ridder chain were sold in 2006. The *Inquirer* and *Daily News* were purchased by McClatchy chain, but it quickly ditched their high overhead by selling both papers for $550 million to a local investor group called Philadelphia Media Holdings (PMH).

PMH idn't realize it at the time, but it had bitten off more than it could chew. Its investors appointed Brian Tierney, a local public relations company executive, to be publisher of both the *Inquirer* and *Daily News*. When Chris Satullo decided to take another job at the paper, Tierney promoted me to replace him as editorial page editor. He also doubled my department's annual freelance budget to $500,000, which allowed me to contract former *Inquirer* reporters Mark Bowden, author of *Black Hawk Down*, and H. G. "Buzz" Bissinger, author of *Friday Night Lights*, to be contributing columnists.

Tierney had long been active in Republican politics, so it was no surprise when he also said he wanted more conservative voices in the paper. He asked me to give freelance contracts to Rick Santorum, who was a former Republican US senator, and John Yoo, who served as an assistant attorney general in President George W. Bush's administration.

Tierney touted Yoo as a Philly guy because he grew up in the city after being born in Seoul, Korea. He ignored the fact that it was Yoo who wrote the infamous waterboarding memos that Bush used to justify the torture of accused jihadist terrorists. The *Inquirer*'s largely left-leaning readership vigorously objected to our hiring Yoo, which prompted the *New York Times* to write about the controversy. I bit my lip but defended our contract with Yoo, arguing that his occasional columns helped promote "further discourse, which is the objective of newspaper commentary."

In reality, the only comfort I found in publishing either Yoo or Santorum was in Tierney's agreement to also let me hire George Curry, publisher of the politically liberal *Emerge* magazine, which became famous in a 1996 for a cover that depicted Supreme Court Justice Clarence Thomas as a lawn jockey. The illustration's caption read "Uncle Thomas." I knew George, a fellow Alabamian, from conventions of the NABJ and was delighted to have his particular perspective published regularly in the *Inquirer*.

The Yoo controversy eventually resolved itself after my freelance budget was cut drastically when the *Inquirer* became overwhelmed by debt. Like other newspapers across America, it and *Daily News* were trying desperately to withstand devastating revenue losses as a flood of readers and advertisers abandoned print publications for websites. The local investors group finally surrendered in 2010 and in an auction sold the *Inquirer*, *Daily News*, and Philly.com for the bargain-basement price of $135 million to a hedge fund led by Angelo, Gordon & Co.

Our new owner, which called itself Philadelphia Media Network, did what hedge funds do—slash budgets and cut staffing. The fifteen full-time employees in my department were reduced to seven, including myself, deputy editor Paul Davies, commentary editor Kevin Ferris, foreign affairs columnist Trudy Rubin, and editorial writers Melanie Burney, Cindy Burton, and Russell Cooke. The board's reduced importance was made clear with the reassignments of editorial assistants Pat Sweeney and Pat Mazurek, who had been with our department more than a decade.

Further staff cuts in 2013 forced me to make my toughest personnel decision since firing a reporter when I was the Alabama state editor for United Press International. The *Inquirer*'s executive editor, Stan Wischnowski, told me to choose either Melanie or Cindy to be reassigned to the South Jersey news bureau, which was shorthanded. Melanie and I were the only Black members of the editorial board, but in the end, I chose her.

CHAPTER 26

Because most of our editorials concerned politics, I believed Cindy's past experience as a political reporter was needed more. What I didn't know at the time was that our online readers tended to prefer human interest stories like the ones Melanie wrote when she was an education reporter.

So the same person who five years earlier had asked Melanie to join the board was now letting her go. I could see the hurt in her eyes, but she didn't argue.

Mel went back to Cherry Hill, which is where we first met when she came to that *Inquirer* bureau in 2000 after being an Associated Press reporter for fourteen years. I had come to the South Jersey office a year earlier to create a commentary page for suburban readers. Our mutual wire-service backgrounds led to our friendship, but everyone who knew her was impressed by Melanie's attention to detail whether writing an editorial or planning a birthday party. That's why we called her "the general."

The generous $500,000 freelance budget that our former publisher, Brian Tierney, had given me was slashed to $50,000 by our new hedge-fund owners, who needed to pinch pennies to produce the excessive returns on investment that they had promised shareholders. That meant no more contracts with George Curry, Mark Bowden, Buzz Bissinger, Rick Santorum, or John Yoo.

Even worse, the pressure to increase revenue was so intense that our new publisher, former *Newsweek* president Greg Osberg, angrily forced my deputy editor, Paul Davies, to resign for writing a column that cost the paper money. There was nothing wrong with Paul's column, which criticized the Pennsylvania Convention Center for letting the building trade unions bully it into allowing them to charge excessive fees to set up trade shows. Those fees were costing the convention center business, but instead of admitting that fact, the PCC canceled a half-million-dollar advertising contract with the *Inquirer*.

Osberg told Paul he would be fired unless he accepted a demotion and became a *Daily News* reporter. Paul had been a *Daily News* reporter from 1997 to 2004 and worked for the *Wall Street Journal* and other publications before becoming my deputy in 2007. He decided to quit. That, however, didn't assuage Osberg's wrath.

Blaming me for publishing Paul's column, he directed the *Inquirer*'s executive editor, Stan Wischnowski, to take away my title as editorial page editor but required me to perform the same duties while reporting to Stan. I persuaded Stan to talk Osberg out of taking away my title since I would still be doing the same work. But I was placed on probation and ordered to write a mission statement that more clearly defined my department's goals. "Welcome to corporate America," I thought.

Without a deputy and already shorthanded, I had to stop taking the weeks of vacation I had accrued so others on my staff could take the time off that they had earned. I also never got a raise during the ten years I was editorial page editor, so you can imagine my elation when the hedge fund had finally squeezed as much as it could out of the *Inquirer*, *Daily News*, and Philly.com and sold them in 2012 to another group of local investors called Interstate General Media (IGM). Unfortunately, the new company created new problems for the editorial board.

IGM's principal investors were H. G. "Gerry" Lenfest, who became a billionaire when the suburban cable company he started was sold to Comcast; New York parking garage magnate Lewis Katz, who once owned both the New Jersey Nets basketball team and New Jersey Devils hockey team; and New Jersey insurance executive George E. Norcross III, one of the most powerful behind-the-scenes politicians in the state.

Seeing this rich, politically active trio take over the *Inquirer* was like landing on some multiverse world where nothing was what it should be.

For years our editorial board had criticized Norcross for being the "Boss Tweed" of South Jersey. Now, Norcross was my boss. Almost topping that, the first time I was introduced to Katz, he accused me of being rude to him sometime in the past because I refused to take a telephone call from his office to discuss a business project that our editorial board opposed. Having absolutely no recollection of what he was talking about, all I could do was apologize. From that inglorious beginning, the editorial board seemed always on the defensive with our new owners.

Our new publisher was Bob Hall, who was also the *Inquirer*'s publisher before it was sold by Knight Ridder in 2006. I was verbally reprimanded by Hall in 2013 for writing a column that asked readers to write letters protesting his decision to stop publishing the *Inquirer*'s daily op-ed page. The column noted that it was only section of the *Inquirer* set aside primarily for commentaries that were not written by staff members. I remain convinced that my being chewed out by Hall was orchestrated by Norcross, who in his new role could retaliate in any way he pleased to the board's past criticism of his Machiavellian politics. But the retribution didn't stop there.

A few months later, the "Opinion" tab on Philly.com, which gave readers access to *Inquirer* editorials and commentaries, was removed. I was worried

CHAPTER 26

because online readership was closely monitored, and those statistics were used to determine each department's budget and staffing. I found out later from data provided to me surreptitiously that our readership was still much higher than that of several news departments whose online presence had not been sabotaged.

It wasn't until another ownership change in 2014 that we got the print op-ed page back and "Opinion" was restored as a tab on Philly.com. The board celebrated with a candle-adorned cake. But my tenure as editorial page editor continued to be a struggle.

Every staff cut, budget reduction, and perceived slight made me more determined to keep our board from being dismissed as an anachronistic relic. I pushed my staff to embrace the *Inquirer*'s new "digital first" mantra and volunteered us to test drive each online production innovation the paper wanted to try. With each new reduction in print production jobs, I assumed copyediting and page design duties that editors at my level didn't typically handle. I sized headlines, changed fonts, digitally placed photos and cartoons, and, like copy boys of old, passed out pages for proofreading.

It was two years after Paul was forced to resign when I finally received permission to fill the vacant deputy editor position. I promoted our op-ed page editor, Josh Gohlke, an excellent reporter, writer, editor, and formidable grammarian. If Josh had one weakness, it was his inability to avoid butting heads with our foreign affairs columnist, Trudy Rubin, over her use of State Department jargon or other words that Josh deemed inappropriate for a general audience. Josh's battles with Trudy reminded me of how I avoided a similar situation when, only eight years after graduating from college, I became United Press International's state news editor in Alabama.

My UPI staff included veteran political reporter Bessie Ford, who, by the time I became her boss, had covered the governor and legislature politics in Montgomery for more than a dozen years. Bessie had a reputation for not suffering fools, but I found her perfectly fine to work with so long as I deferred to her news judgment on subjects that she obviously knew more about than I did.

Correspondingly, Bessie never questioned my authority, nor did she ever object to my making suggestions or asking questions about the work she turned in. It's called mutual respect, and it works every time you can find it. Unfortunately, that's not always easy in journalism or in life. I think Josh, like me, learned patience can be a virtue when persistence is your foe.

CHAPTER 27

ABROAD IN ETHIOPIA AND CHINA

Despite the *Inquirer*'s seeming hopelessly perched on a trembling cliff overlooking economic calamity, I was able to make two overseas trips during my ten years as editorial page editor. Those visits to Asia and Africa provided two distinctly different views of the world that made me both appreciate and question what I see in my own country.

In 2010 I accompanied a team of American doctors and nurses sent to Ethiopia by the Healing the Children organization, which since 1979 has provided otherwise unattainable medical care to children around the world. My wife, Denice, a registered nurse, was on a team from the South Jersey and Philadelphia region that performed pediatric surgeries and provided other medical services at the two main hospitals in Addis Ababa: Black Lion and CURE.

I spent most of my time researching two articles I planned to write by observing the medical team, taking photographs of the young patients, and interviewing their parents. It was inspiring to see how hard the doctors and nurses worked and sobering to see what they had to work with, especially at the older Black Lion Hospital, where much of the medical equipment looked as if it had been there since hospital was founded in 1964.

Michael Ritchey, a pediatric surgeon from Phoenix, Arizona, admitted the challenge seemed daunting, but he expressed sympathy for Ethiopia's physicians, who performed their duties every day amid such conditions. "There are

CHAPTER 27

so many patients and so few specialists, and these specialists have few resources, so they can't care for all the patients they see," said Ritchey.

Many of the children at Lion had tumors in their larynx and on their vocal cords, which began growing when the human papillomavirus was transferred to them at birth from their mothers. Removing the tumors requires a tracheotomy, but that somewhat simple procedure in the United States can be dangerous for children in Ethiopia, who risk infection once they return to their homes sometimes hundreds of miles from Addis Ababa.

That risk led many parents to make Black Lion Hospital their home, sometimes for years, so their children could continue receiving treatment for respiratory papillomatosis. The seven-hundred-bed hospital somehow manages to house these families on its grounds. I spoke to Solomon Tenodros, twenty-five, whose two-year-old son, Isac, was a patient. "I don't know how long Isac must stay here," Solomon said. "The first concern is to save the life of my son. I am always here for Isac."

Being of no practical use when the medical team was doing its work, I had plenty of time to see Addis Ababa when I wasn't being a reporter. I mostly walked the streets of the city, usually with one of the entrepreneurial young men who waited outside the Sheraton hotel complex and charged tourists a modest price to be their tour guides. Addis Ababa was both modern city and rural village, with wide paved streets filled with taxis intersecting narrow dirt-covered roads with chickens and goats scurrying across them. Present on both were women and girls of all ages carrying bundles of the sticks on their backs to be used as fuel inside their homes.

Street corners buzzed with men selling khat leaves, a legal stimulant in Ethiopia and other Horn of Africa countries. Other vendors barked out the prices of the goods in their carts, everything from meats served with injera bread to fashionable clothing to compact discs of Tizita or Ethio-jazz music. My guide suggested a place to buy a present for Denice and took me to a garage where the apparent proprietor offered me a Fanta orange soda as we sat outside and looked at jewelry he was selling. With a US dollar worth about fifty Ethiopian birr, it was easy to strike a bargain.

The first of my two commentaries about Ethiopia concerned Healing the Children's medical mission, while the second explored the three-thousand-year-old nation's current political climate. I interviewed a senior embassy official who requested anonymity about Ethiopia's role in the war on terror, which had spread to neighboring countries where Al-Shabaab and ISIS groups were located. I also met with students at Addis Ababa University students who expressed love for their country but criticized the autocratic nature of its democratic government.

Just like students I met years later in China, the Ethiopian students said their success hinged on joining the country's ruling party at that time, the Ethiopian People's Revolutionary Democratic Front. A young teacher taking a post-graduate class said it was dangerous to question the government too much. "We are encouraged to speak our minds, but if you do you may lose your job, or you may not get a salary increase or promotion," she said.

"There are spies everywhere," an Ethiopian journalist told me. "There are people who report on other people." "So much for democracy," I thought. But with terrorist groups harbored in neighboring Sudan, Somalia, Eritrea, and Yemen, America has been more than happy to give Ethiopia's repressive government a free pass in exchange for allyship. The State Department official I interviewed at the US embassy said I shouldn't judge Ethiopia's government without putting it in perspective. "Less than twenty years ago, Ethiopia was ruled by a brutal communist regime," he said.

That sentiment was echoed by university professor Abiyi Ford, whose parents emigrated from the United States to Ethiopia with the Marcus Garvey movement in the 1920s. Ford said Ethiopia's limits on freedom of speech were comparable to America's prohibition against yelling "fire" in a crowded theater. "It depends on how and what you are saying in criticizing the government," Ford said. "The topography of Ethiopia's history is full of land mines, any one of which could go boom!"

I wasn't persuaded that Ethiopia's government had to be as repressive as it was simply because of its past but agreed that the situation required context. Ruled by an emperor, Haile Selassie, from 1930 until 1974, and then by a communist military junta, Ethiopia didn't have an elected government until 1995. American democracy wasn't what it should have been when it was that young either. In fact, our nearly 250-year-old government still struggles to truly represent all of its citizens, but that doesn't mean it shouldn't give Ethiopia more than a nudge toward a more democratic system.

Four years after my Ethiopia trip, I was part of a delegation with three journalists from the *Los Angeles Times*, *Chicago Tribune*, and *Huffington Post* who were invited to China by the Hong Kong-based China-US Exchange Foundation. In Beijing, Shanghai, and Xi'an, we met government officials, entrepreneurs, academics, students, and even a few farmers on a side trip to the

CHAPTER 27

tiny village of Da Ping, population one hundred. All expressed their fervent belief that China's participation in the world market—not its military prowess—is crucial to its success.

College students I met in Beijing seemed annoyed that we Americans couldn't see that their country's autocratic mixture of communism and capitalism best served the Chinese people. They proudly acknowledged that Communist Party membership was a crucial prerequisite to unlocking the door to whatever career goals they had, government or corporate.

Fu Ying, China's vice minister of foreign affairs, was the highest-ranking government official to meet with our delegation. The former ambassador to the United Kingdom repeated the message we kept hearing from other Chinese people—they didn't see themselves as America's enemy or competitor, but as a trade partner. She insisted democracy and human rights were "taking root" in her country but said we shouldn't expect China to "copy and paste" what the Western world does.

In Shanghai, we met venture capitalist Eric X. Li, founder of Chengwei Capital, who said China flourishes because it puts the good of the "collective" above the individual. Li said meritocracy works better in China than in America because its public schools are better. Only the rich can afford the type of education needed to excel in America, he said.

Outside Shanghai in Pudong, our group visited Huawei Technologies, which designs and develops telecommunications equipment exported to 140 countries, but not to the United States, which has accused Huawei of designing products that provided the Chinese government unauthorized access to American communication networks.

The Huawei officials we met insisted their competition for market superiority was not political. I remembered that four years later, when Huawei's chief financial officer, Meng Wanzhou, was detained in Canada at the request of the United States after her company was accused of violating US sanctions by selling products to Iran. She wasn't allowed to return to China for three years until the United States withdrew its extradition request.

The sprawling Huawei complex was an architectural marvel designed to house eight thousand workers. But even more impressive was the Chinese version of Silicon Valley that was being built near Xi'an, which is where archaeologists in 1974 discovered an army of life-size terra-cotta soldiers that had been entombed around 209 BC by Qin Shi Huang, China's first emperor. Only a few miles from the mausoleum where the thousands of clay soldiers stand guard, companies including Oracle, Bosch, Siemens, Fujitsu, and others were creating technological innovations.

That version of China is far different from the parts of China the rest of the world rarely sees. That's where you will find the more than two hundred million among its population of 1.4 billion who live in poverty. We visited some of them in Da Ping, a tiny village on Mount Huashan about ninety minutes from Xi'an. There are no jobs in Da Ping, so most of its young people had left. The village's few remaining residents grew cabbages for subsistence and shared a pit that served as a communal latrine.

Even so, the villagers we interviewed proudly introduced us to the one baby in town, a beautiful little girl maybe six months old. Looking at the child, I thought to myself that her home would one day fade from existence, just like the morning mists that covered the mountains surrounding the village. Asked if he'd ever thought of leaving Da Ping, an elderly man said through an interpreter, "We like our clean air."

Days later, while inhaling the polluted air of Beijing, I understood what he meant. It would have been nice to see Tiananmen Square when it and Beijing's skyscrapers weren't obscured by low-hanging smog. Of course, America, too, has been known to skirt pollution and other rules in the name of progress. But, with its mixture of capitalism and communism, China changes the rules at a whim, mostly for the sake of efficiency. I left China wondering how many more years would pass before its people decided they want more freedom.

CHAPTER 28

NEED TO GET OUT OF PHILLY, AGAIN

Any hopes of doing more reporting overseas faded amid the *Inquirer*'s continued financial problems. Two of the paper's three owners, Lewis Katz and George Norcross, were openly arguing two years into their purchase, and in 2014, they and the third owner, Gerry Lenfest, decided to end their triumvirate with a silent auction—winner takes all. Katz and Lenfest joined forces to make a successful $88 million bid.

Tragically, less than a week after the auction, Katz was killed in a plane crash. His family then sold their stake in the *Inquirer*, *Philadelphia Daily News*, and Philly.com to Lenfest, who became our sole owner. But two years later, Lenfest donated the company to a nonprofit he created—the Lenfest Institute. His move was designed to keep the two newspapers and website in business even as print journalism was dying and, presumably, after his own death, which occurred four years later, when he was eighty-eight.

I liked Lenfest. I remember our first meeting after I became editorial page editor in 2007. He wanted the editorial board to support construction of the Museum of the American Revolution in Philadelphia, which didn't get built until 2017. After the meeting, Lenfest pulled me aside to let me know that although everyone called him Gerry, his given name, like his father's, was also Harold. A tall man with bushy eyebrows and a ready smile, he always came across as someone's grandfather, albeit a very rich one.

I thought my job might become more secure with the renamed Lenfest

Institute as the *Inquirer*'s owner. "No more meddling by avaricious hedge funds, egotistical businessmen, or political bosses bent on revenge," I thought. But I had not anticipated a different threat. The institute's board decided in 2017 to further consolidate the operations of the *Inquirer* and *Daily News* by combining their editorial boards under a newly created managing editor for opinion position. I was told by executive editor Stan Wischnowski that both *Daily News* editorial page editor Sandy Shea and I were being considered for the position.

I thought I would get the job, primarily because Sandy's much smaller operation at the *Daily News* did not require her to gain the same level of print and digital skills that I needed to produce additional content for both the *Inquirer* and Philly.com. I also thought that my being editorial page editor of what was considered the paper of record in Philadelphia would matter, but it didn't.

I was stunned when Stan told me Sandy was getting the job. He hemmed and hawed but never articulated exactly what journalistic or other skills made Sandy the superior candidate. I think Stan also must have forgotten that he once told me in a casual conversation months ago, before the new position was announced, that he and his wife considered Sandy a friend with whom they occasionally had dinner.

I also believe that while I was hustling to produce the more extensive print and digital versions of the *Inquirer* opinion sections, Sandy's lighter production schedule had allowed her to develop relationships that I didn't have with Lenfest Institute board members who may have had input in Stan's decision. Maybe I was just a victim of corporate politics, but I felt as if I was back in Alabama in the 1960s, when a Black man's hard work didn't mean a thing to some white folks. He was still just a nigger.

It didn't help that I knew most of the work I did to produce copy for the *Inquirer*'s opinion pages and online was handled in Sandy's stead by a copyeditor. I also knew that despite my being a target of two publishers after the *Inquirer* fell into bankruptcy—Greg Osberg and Bob Hall—neither they nor anyone else had ever questioned my dedication or complained about the quality of my work.

Yet, after keeping our department operating at an elevated level despite staff and budget cuts, not taking accrued vacations, and not receiving a single pay raise in ten years, I was rewarded with what amounted to a demotion.

My job title was downgraded from "editor" to "editorial page manager," and my office was taken away. But my actual duties changed very little for

CHAPTER 28

months, until Sandy hired a deputy editor to do that work. After that, Sandy seemed to think it best to remind me at every opportunity that I was now her subordinate, which I actually appreciated.

Her treatment reminded me of advice I had given so many others over the years. When you no longer find joy coming to work, it's time to move on.

I was tempted to call Dick Sprague, an attorney I knew casually who years earlier successfully represented a reporter who sued the *Inquirer* for unfair treatment, but I decided against it.

I remembered an experience in the 1970s when I asked the US Justice Department to file suit on my behalf against a Birmingham apartment building owner who insisted he had no dwellings for rent a day after a white friend told me he had just given notice that he was leaving the same complex. The US attorneys told me they needed to show a pattern of racism, not a single incident, to make a successful case.

But the bigger reason I decided not to sue the *Inquirer* for discrimination was my loyalty and affection for the newspaper. The *Inky* gave me my first job outside Birmingham in 1985, and I discovered I was capable of being a good journalist in a much bigger city. Fourteen years later, when I needed a spot to land so I could leave the *Baltimore Sun*, the *Inky* again hired me and put me on a path to become the 194-year-old newspaper's first Black editorial page editor—a position I held for ten years.

I didn't want to sue the paper, but I needed to leave it. The question was where I would go?

CHAPTER 29

LOST FAITH IN MY CHURCH, NOT GOD

Feeling betrayed by the *Inquirer* wasn't the only reason Denice and I started thinking we should move again. We liked South Jersey, with its tolerable summers and winters, lovely falls and springs, short distance to the Jersey Shore, and manageable traffic and affordability. But more than all that, we loved our church—until we didn't.

We began attending Trinity Christian Chapel about a year after we moved to South Jersey in 2018. The Christian and Missionary Alliance–affiliated church wasn't our first choice. It had fewer than two hundred members, maybe six of them people of color. And while Denice's family were members of a Church of Christ congregation in Kansas City, I had been a Presbyterian since childhood.

We first visited Bunker Hill Presbyterian Church in Washington Township, but like many mainstream churches across America, it's low attendance suggested it was dying on the vine. Then one day our neighbors Jim and Judy Estes invited us to Trinity. We were immediately struck by the friendliness of the people we met. None of that saccharine, brotherly love stuff you get visiting some churches, which too often ends when people get into their cars to go home.

The handshakes at Trinity were genuine. People looked you in the eye, and they didn't just ask how you were doing; they asked if they could do anything for you. In addition to Sunday services, we started going to weekday Bible

CHAPTER 29

studies, get-acquainted dinners, picnics, and other events. Over the next fifteen years or so, I served several terms as a deacon and Denice as a deaconess.

We loved Trinity and its people. The church's mission to spread the Gospel seemed sacrosanct, and we gladly became a part of it. Everything expressed from the pulpit was Bible based, with hardly any references to current political issues. The church was a huge supporter of overseas ministries, which made sense since most Christian and Missionary Alliance churches are in foreign countries.

It was clear from the beginning of our attendance that most of Trinity's members were pro-life, but the church's emphasis was always on helping women considering abortion. It collected funds for a local Choices of the Heart counseling center, which stressed that it provided "confidential and non-judgmental services to men and women regarding your pregnancy and sexual health."

I don't recall any sermons from Trinity's pulpit demonizing abortion providers or pro-choice politicians before 2006. That's when our pastor resigned and was replaced by a minister who emphasized evangelism, spreading the Gospel to save souls, but eventually seemed to get caught up in the political movement that, to its glee, discovered the abortion issue could be exploited to gain support among evangelical Christians.

Under our new pastor, Denice and I joined other Trinity members in handing out religious tracts in malls, parks, and other public spaces, leaving church invitations on the doorknobs of homes, and passing out cash gift certificates at grocery stores while inviting the recipients to come to our church. But even as we focused on evangelism, our pastor's sermons increasingly made references to abortion and his belief that the Democratic Party was an accessory to its continuation.

That accusation grew more frequent and harsher after the election of President Barack Obama in 2008. "Faith changes us. I know it changed me," Obama said after becoming president. "It renews in us a sense of possibility. It allows us to believe that although we are all sinners, and that at times we will falter, there's always the possibility of redemption." Such words didn't matter to our pastor. His focus seemed to swing more toward saving babies than saving souls, and the nation's first Black president became a lightning rod for his derision.

Of course, Trinity wasn't the only mostly white evangelical church that similarly believed pro-choice Democrats who also supported gay rights had put America on a highway to hell. Even now, congregations across the nation

LOST FAITH IN MY CHURCH, NOT GOD

continue to be manipulated by largely amoral politicians who care more about getting elected than about providing a health-care system that might help more women considering abortion to choose life.

As bothered as Denice and I were by some of our pastor's off-the-cuff remarks during sermons, we were hurt more when church members we considered friends agreed with him. That included the widow of a man whose generosity of spirit convinced us that Trinity was the right church for us. Apparently thinking Trinity members shared not only the same faith but the same politics, she spoke so derisively of Obama after church one Sunday that Denice and I could only walk away. I wondered how such an intelligent woman could be so sorely misguided.

Prior to Obama's election, I wrote a column for the *Inquirer* headlined "When Faith and Politics Overlap" that expressed my growing discomfort with my church. Some church members were forwarding mass emails they'd received from political groups that said it would be "un-Christian" to vote for any pro-choice candidate.

The emails briefly stopped after our pastor asked people to stop sending them, but they resumed as the election got closer. One included a video of Black independent presidential candidate Alan Keyes, who accused Obama of "infanticide." Another included a link to a social media post titled "Why I Can't Vote for Obama," written by a Black man who described himself as a "fabulous concert pianist" and "man of God." "Many of my friends process their identity through their blackness; I process my identity through Christ," he said.

Given that both Keyes and the "fabulous concert pianist" were Black, I assumed their emails were circulated among our congregation by someone with me in mind. Maybe they concluded I was also pro-choice after reading in a 2008 column I wrote that I had changed my opposition to gay marriage after learning how much my brother Calvin's partner did for him when he was dying of AIDS. The column concluded that since civil union laws don't provide the same rights as marriage does, and since marriages do not have to be performed by clergy to be legal, a religious standard shouldn't be universally applied for any couple to marry.

"My church would not marry same-sex couples and should not be forced to by government edict. But, to me, that doesn't mean gay couples should be denied a nonreligious marriage," I said. "Neither I nor my church would recognize them as married under God, but they don't care about us. They care

CHAPTER 29

about getting the taxation, insurance, and government-services benefits of being a legal pair.

"Some would argue that to condone same-sex marriage in any form is to condone sin. I am no theologian, no preacher, but I do believe that we all sin, and that all who don't repent and put their faith in Christ for salvation will face the same fate. That's gospel."

Obama's defeat of John McCain in the 2008 election didn't stop the Republican Party from continuing to exploit evangelical Christians by hammering the new president's pro-choice and gay rights positions. More emails were circulated among Trinity members, including some with links to a Family Research Council website that featured interviews with Black ministers. "Homosexuality is a choice, and skin color is not a choice, so there is no comparison of the two," said an Arlington, Texas, pastor.

Even though George W. Bush, a Republican, was president when the recession began in 2007, voters punished Democrats in the 2010 midterm elections by giving the GOP control of the House and reducing Democrats' advantage in the Senate to fifty-one of one hundred seats. Smelling blood, Republicans continued to recruit evangelical leaders by portraying Obama and any other Democrat running for office as unworthy of Christian support.

And despite his reputation as a womanizing hedonist with ethically questionable business practices, Donald Trump leveraged evangelical support as the Republican presidential nominee to help him defeat Hillary Clinton in the 2016 election. Trump's promise to appoint pro-life Supreme Court justices was the decisive factor for many conservative Christians who blindly believed a court ruling could do what has never been done in the history of the world—end all abortions.

I pointed out in a column after Trump's inauguration that abortion is referenced at least as far back as the Bible's Book of Numbers, which says an adulterous woman shall be "made to drink the water that brings a curse and causes bitter suffering, it will enter her, her abdomen will swell, and her womb will miscarry." If the antiabortion movement's aim is fewer abortions, I said, it should shift from being pro-life to pro-child.

"Instead of evangelicals putting their faith in the power of politicians or Supreme Court justices to shut down abortion clinics, they should push for pro-child public policies and programs that would not only help pregnant women make the right choice but provide readily available and adequate assistance to rear children in safe, healthy, nurturing environments."

While I found it easy to express my views on abortion and gay rights in a newspaper column written for a general audience, I never found the nerve to speak my mind with other Trinity members. I didn't want to argue with people I loved as fellow Christians. Nor did I want them to see me as that "good nigger," to use A. G. Gaston's words, who white folks tolerated because he didn't make them feel uncomfortable about being racists.

My chosen silence became intolerable, however, when I realized it allowed Trinity's Trump supporters to assume I was a fellow traveler. Denice and I decided confronting the Trumpsters with the truth would likely produce the same outcome as would our leaving the church without getting into arguments, so without saying why, we simply stopped going to Trinity.

The decision was hard; I was born again at Trinity. First baptized when I was eleven at Westminster Presbyterian Church in Birmingham, I was baptized again more than forty years later at Trinity—not because I needed to do it a second time to ensure my place in heaven, but because I wanted to demonstrate how much that little church had strengthened my faith in God. Too bad I lost faith in it.

Given what had happened at Trinity and my demotion at the *Inquirer*, Denice and I decided that God was telling us to find another church, and He was also telling us to find it in greener pastures.

CHAPTER 30

FINAL LANDING SPOT, HOUSTON

My grand plan had always been to return to Birmingham to work in the newspaper industry a few more years before retiring in my hometown. I looked forward to reuniting with my childhood friend Charles Abron, who had retired after more than twenty years in the Navy. Denice's best friend, Theresa Swain, and her husband, Mike, were in Birmingham too. "It is time to make my plan a reality," I thought, obliviously forgetting that wanting something to happen doesn't mean it will.

My grand plan was dashed by the reality that one Birmingham newspaper, the *Post-Herald*, had ceased operation more than fifteen years earlier, and the other paper, the *Birmingham News*, was cutting print jobs, not adding them, as it hastened its transition into a digital-only publication. I began considering alternative final stops, and at the top of the list was Houston, which was where our son, Dennis, lived with his wife, Andrea, a native of that city.

I called the *Houston Chronicle*'s managing editor, Vernon Loeb, who was a former *Inquirer* assistant managing editor. I kept checking back with Vernon over the next six months, stressing that I would take any job within reason to leave the *Inquirer*. Finally, he called me one day with news that the *Chronicle*'s editorial page editor, Jeff Cohen, was retiring and that he would mention me as a possible replacement. I was happy but, considering my *Inquirer* experience, not sure I wanted to be an editorial page editor again.

In the end, it didn't matter. The *Chronicle* decided not to take a chance on someone so unfamiliar with Texas and instead chose Lisa Falkenberg, its Pulitzer Prize–winning metro columnist, to succeed Cohen. Then, Lisa, perhaps urged by Vernon, hired me to be a senior editorial writer. Goodbye, Philly!

I actually already knew Lisa, having served with her as a Pulitzer Prize juror for editorial writing in 2016. Our board also included Doug Miller, Andrea White, Jim Newkirk, the only other African American on the board, and deputy editorial page editor Evan Mintz. I first met Jim when he and I were on the Pulitzer jury that selected Lisa to receive the 2015 prize for commentary. Jim recused himself whenever Lisa's entry was being discussed, but the rest of the jury agreed that Lisa's columns exposing abuses in Texas's criminal trial system were deserving.

My new grand plan was to try to work five years at the *Chronicle* before retiring at age seventy. Unfortunately, less than two years into the job, I knew that was unlikely to happen. Having several years earlier embraced the *Inquirer*'s aggressive and necessary transition from an old-fashioned newspaper to a digital-first publication, I was dismayed by the *Chronicle*'s rather lackadaisical attempts to escape becoming just another ink-stained dinosaur failing to escape extinction.

I blamed the *Chronicle*'s lack of urgency on its operating in a bubble created by its owner, the Hearst Corporation, which, unlike the *Inquirer*'s financially struggling owners, was better able to withstand its losses. Hearst was the owner in whole or part of a diversity of companies that included more than twenty newspapers besides the *Chronicle*, almost as many magazines, thirty TV stations, and the A&E and ESPN cable TV networks.

Lisa seemed receptive whenever I suggested digital strategies we had used at the *Inquirer* to increase the editorial board's online readership, but very little changed. The same thing happened, or didn't happen, when I made suggestions to update the *Chronicle*'s print opinion pages. It was maddening to find out the newspaper of record in the nation's fourth-largest city didn't have a dedicated Sunday opinion section for editorials and commentaries. Instead, that content was buried inside a section reserved for national news stories culled from wire services.

Despite my irritation with seeing my suggestions merely tolerated, I liked my job, until I received a negative employee evaluation from Lisa, which concluded that I didn't get out of the office enough. Perhaps her criticism was meant to provide incentive for me to get to know Houston better, but after doing the reporting necessary to write editorials that touched on aspects of

CHAPTER 30

Houston life ranging from stray dogs biting schoolchildren to why the city had competing Martin Luther King Jr. Day parades, I thought I was doing well enough not to receive a negative evaluation.

Then it dawned on me that Lisa's attitude toward me was comparable to how I felt when I became the *Inquirer*'s editorial page editor eleven years earlier. I wanted to run my board my way, not the way someone else suggested I should. I thought about how I would have felt if my predecessor at the *Inquirer* had remained on the editorial board and kept offering "helpful" suggestions. I decided I didn't want Lisa to think I wanted her to run the board my way, but I also didn't want to follow her suggestion and hit the streets of Houston, as I had in Baltimore twenty years earlier, to get to know the city better.

I knew then that it was time to retire, and in January 2022, I did. My forty-five-year career as a newspaperman was over.

CHAPTER 31

PAID TO WRITE WHAT I BELIEVE

The highest point of my journalism career was winning a Pulitzer Prize, but near the top of my list of favorite memories is guiding the *Inquirer*'s 2008 endorsement of Barack Obama to become this country's first Black president. Many of our conservative readers expected "a liberal rag," which is what some called us, to endorse any Democrat out of habit, but they were wrong about our endorsement record, and they were ignoring that our new publisher, former advertising company executive Brian Tierney, was active in Pennsylvania Republican politics.

Brian showed little interest in the state primary contest between Obama and Hillary Clinton, but I feared he would insist on endorsing GOP frontrunner John McCain in the general election. I was actually leaning more toward endorsing Clinton before the primary. After all, Obama was a little-known freshman senator from Illinois, while Clinton already knew as much as her husband, Bill, about being president from spending eight years as one of his key advisers.

I also I worried that Obama, with a white mother, Kenyan father, and childhood spent mostly in Hawaii and Indonesia, didn't know what it's like to grow up Black in America. I addressed my reservations in an earlier *Inquirer* column that compared Obama's 2008 campaign with Jesse Jackson's 1984 run for president, which wasn't supported by Black mayors Wilson Goode of Philadelphia, Andrew Young of Atlanta, and Richard Arrington Jr. of Birmingham, or by civil rights heroine Coretta Scott King.

CHAPTER 31

"It is not that Obama has to prove he's an African American by ancestry; his father was Kenyan, his mother a white woman from Kansas. It is not that Obama has to prove that his beige skin color is dark enough; African Americans come in all shades—ebony to ivory and everything in between," I wrote.

But this last point, in making clear that Blackness isn't really about color, brings us closer to what Blackness is and whether Obama is truly Black. You see, in the United States "Black" is merely a construct developed centuries ago to identify a group of people designated for oppression—through slavery, segregation, or less overt discrimination.

Black means *oppressed*.

So, when other African Americans wonder if Obama is Black enough, they're really questioning whether he has been oppressed enough. Does he think like a person whose great-grandparents may have been slaves, whose grandparents, and parents, through statute and code, were treated as inferior? Does the fact that Obama spent so much of his childhood in foreign countries mean that he doesn't see racial issues in quite the same way as those of us who grew up here?

My questions weren't answered, but I felt much better about Obama after he was forced to confront the issue of race in a May 18, 2008, speech at the National Constitution Center in Philadelphia. I say "forced" because Obama seemed content to let people assume they understood his views on race until news coverage of his presidential campaign began mentioning a 2003 sermon by his former pastor and mentor in Chicago, the Reverend Jeremiah A. Wright. Discussing the plight of African Americans, Wright said, "The government gives them the drugs, builds bigger prisons, passes a three-strike law, and then wants us to sing 'God Bless America.' No, no, no, not God bless America. God damn America."

Obama needed to respond. He needed to let Black people know he didn't necessarily disagree with Wright's depiction of racism, but at the same time, he needed to reassure white folks that, warts and all, he loved his country.

"I chose to run for president at this moment in history because I believe deeply that we cannot solve the challenges of our time unless we solve them together," he said, "unless we perfect our union by understanding that we may have different stories, but we hold common hopes; that we may not look the same and we may not have come from the same place, but we all want to move in the same direction—toward a better future for our children and our grandchildren."

It was a magnificent speech, but even with the *Inquirer*'s endorsement, Obama lost the Pennsylvania primary to Clinton by ten points. I remained skeptical that he could win the general election in November and said so in a column that June. "Friends of mine can't understand my cynicism about Barack Obama's quest to become the first African American president. They're sniffing the air like it smells of jubilee, while I'm moping around like Eeyore, the perpetually pessimistic donkey." The column mentioned a white West Virginia woman who told reporters she wouldn't vote for Obama because "Black people have always given white people trouble."

I became more optimistic, however, as Election Day approached and was fully in Obama's corner when the editorial board met with Tierney to decide whom the paper would endorse. After hearing only one board member speak in favor of McCain, Tierney reluctantly agreed to endorse Obama—but with a caveat. We had to also publish an editorial beneath our Obama endorsement that extolled the virtues of John McCain. Not wanting to risk losing the Obama endorsement, I agreed. The *New York Times* noted the discordance in a October 21, 2008, article headlined "Endorsement Dissent at the *Inquirer*."

My column a week after Obama's subsequent victory said, "A dream that has been deferred for more than 100 years exploded into reality last week with the election of Barack Obama, an African American, to become president of the United States." I said his becoming president was the fulfilment of a dream that Black children like me who went to segregated schools were encouraged to have by teachers who taught us to believe anything is possible if you work hard. "And every child of every hue and circumstance should be encouraged to take note."

I frequently urged schools to teach Black history and to ensure that white students understood it was just as important for them to learn as it was for their Black classmates. That is especially true now, with too many conservative politicians labeling Black history as "critical race theory" without being able to define what that term even means.

Historian Carter G. Woodson didn't worry about white students when he created Negro History Week in 1926. His goal was to help Black children take greater pride in their ancestors. But integration has put white and Black students in the same classrooms, which means Black history lessons and African American History Month should be changed accordingly.

CHAPTER 31

I said in a 2008 column that "instead of just studying Crispus Attucks, Sojourner Truth, Booker T. Washington, W. E. B. DuBois, etc., have students spend extra a time on the 'three-fifths clause' in the Constitution, the Kansas-Nebraska Act, the *Dred Scott* decision, the Emancipation Proclamation, the Hayes-Tilden Compromise, the Niagara Movement, the *Brown* decision, the Southern Christian Leadership Conference." Focusing on significant events rather than famous people would also make it easier to note the impactful roles that white people other than Abraham Lincoln have played in improving the status of Black people in America.

Among them is President Harry S. Truman, whose 1948 executive order desegregating America's armed forces was just as important as the 1964 Civil Rights Act and 1965 Voting Rights Act. Truman's directive allowed thousands of Black enlisted men and women to return "to their hometowns determined to gain in civilian life some semblance of the unbiased opportunities the military had provided."

I said history teachers should spend more time talking about what Reconstruction was supposed to accomplish and explaining why it failed. Teach students lessons that cover the first Black members of Congress: Hiram Revels of Mississippi, Benjamin S. Turner of Alabama, Jefferson F. Long of Georgia, Josiah T. Walls of Florida, and Robert C. De Large, Robert Brown Elliott, and Joseph H. Rainey of South Carolina. Elliott's speeches helped spur passage of the 1875 Civil Rights Act, but his and the other Black men's political careers ended when Reconstruction died.

Sadly, these Black heroes are largely forgotten today while statues and even the very names of some universities continue to pay homage to Confederate traitors. I lamented that reality in a 2011 *Inquirer* column that recalled a reporting assignment of mine seventeen years earlier. In Biloxi to research Mississippi's casino gambling industry for the *Baltimore Sun*, I decided to visit Beauvoir, the mansion where the Confederacy's president, Jefferson Davis, lived in luxury after the Civil War instead of rotting in a prison. I hoped to see some sign of Davis's mentality when he tried to preserve an economic system based on the capture, sale, and dehumanization of Black people, but found none among the artifacts on display and trinkets for sale.

My column criticized the twenty-one states, not all of them Southern, planning to commemorate the sesquicentennial of the Confederate attack on Fort Wagner in Charleston that started the Civil War. "Through the end of this year, we will see various attempts to win the history, to obscure the truth that led to the South's secession, to ignore that the Civil War's aftermath included a brutal backlash against Black Americans for having been the catalyst for the South's pain, to glorify soldiers who fought on the wrong side of glory," I said.

Not wanting readers to get the wrong idea about me, I also wrote columns that tried to explain that despite my criticism of our country, I'm actually very patriotic. In a 2007 column, I said, "I can't watch that final charge on Fort Wagner in the movie *Glory* without my eyes getting moist. . . . I believe in the American dream. I also believe a true patriot doesn't hesitate to criticize our nation when it is wrong. If you truly love your country, you want it to be above criticism, and that can only happen when it corrects its imperfections."

I had that same mindset when I wrote a 2001 column asking all Americans to treat Martin Luther King Jr. Day like the national holiday it is and not just a Black holiday. The column referenced a 1962 speech by King when he said, "We are simply seeking to bring into full realization the American dream, a dream yet unfilled. . . . When it is realized, the jangling discords of our nation will be transformed into a beautiful symphony of brotherhood, and men everywhere will know that America is truly the land of the free and the home of the brave."

Many times I wrote about the absolute failure of America's criminal justice system, including in 2014 after the unnecessary deaths of two unarmed Black men shot by police—Michael Brown in Ferguson, Missouri, and Eric Garner in New York. In support of the demonstrators protesting how the men were killed, I said, "Their struggle is for equal justice. That was our parents' struggle, too. It's sad that it also must be our children's struggle, and most likely, their children's as well. The struggle won't end until white police officers and the Black people they are supposed to protect and serve can achieve a higher level of trust."

That doesn't mean police brutality is always a matter of race, which I said in a 2008 column. "The first time I saw police beat a Black man, it was in 1969 in Birmingham, Alabama. No, it's not what you're thinking. The cops were Black too." The victim of that apparent police rage was a teenager who brandished a gun at my high school's annual talent show. He was wrestled to the ground and handcuffed by two Black officers who then proceeded to beat his buttocks with their nightsticks. "Only later did it register with me that in a city infamous for white cops brutalizing Blacks, I had witnessed Black cops exhibiting the same behavior."

CHAPTER 31

That same column mentioned Frank Horn, one of Birmingham's first Black police officers, who grew up a couple of apartments from mine in the Loveman Village housing project. Years later when I interviewed Frank for an article, he told me Birmingham's first Black cops were under constant pressure to prove to the white cops that they, too, were "blue" first.

The Black officers who beat the Black teenager at a Black high school weren't being watched by white cops, so that wasn't their worry. So maybe they were just venting their frustration, or maybe they thought they were giving the kid the type of discipline he should have received at home. That's still no excuse for brutality.

"Police officers have a tough job, and they're only human. They're going to get angry, get frustrated, feel the loss of a comrade. That's expected," I said. "But what's also expected is that if one officer succumbs to his feelings and begins to express them in the treatment of a suspect, his fellow officers will pull him back. When that doesn't happen, when every officer vents his frustrations on a helpless man lying handcuffed on the ground, even if that man has committed a crime, then all you have is a mob, not police officers. And a mob can't be expected to protect the public."

The unjust, disproportionate number of Black people in prison was my topic of choice numerous times. A 2007 column pointed out that Black people were only 13 percent of the US population but 35 percent of the incarcerated. "The racists among us, blatant and closeted, will be quick to attribute the imprisonment disparity to the misguided belief that African Americans are inherently prone to criminality. I've seen no valid studies supporting that view. But numerous scholars have correlated crime to conditions of poverty—and African Americans remain disparately poor.

"Long ago, a convict was actually expected to be rehabilitated in prison. Too many prisons today are little more than warehouses of men and women who become more larcenous and violent there than they were before being locked up," the column said. Noting that Philadelphia's jail was so crowded at the time that inmates were sleeping on concrete floors, I asked readers to "imagine their mood when released." No wonder so many inmates who weren't violent when they entered prison become violent while incarcerated.

I wrote several times about my frustration with the misplaced priorities of my fellow Americans, pointing out in one column that seeking "fairness" isn't necessarily the best way to achieve some goals. "Americans today are preoccupied with what's fair," I said. "It wouldn't be fair, some say, to exclude the richest Americans from an extension of the Bush-era tax cuts. It wouldn't be fair, say others, to give the 12 million immigrants in this country illegally a path to citizenship. And of course, for years affirmative action programs that help erase the vestiges of past discrimination have been derided as unfair.

"Well, you know what? The world isn't fair. Not always anyway. But fair shouldn't even be the goal. Good is always better than fair on any report card I've seen. As a nation, we should want to be good, not merely fair. And being good means making unpalatable choices that place the benefits of the whole above the interests of the few . . . doing that which is good is what America is supposed to be all about."

What's not good, I said in a 2011 column, are vote-hungry politicians who want to reduce funding for social programs that help the very people who need help the most. "I think most Americans want to help the poor. As for those right-wingers who consider themselves religious but want to make budget cuts that hurt the poor, they should read 1 John 3: 17: 'If anyone has material possessions and sees a brother or sister in need but has no pity on them, how can the love of God be in that person?'"

CHAPTER 32

LIFE UNDER THE SUN

Reflecting on a journalism career that spanned parts of five decades, I'm reminded of what Solomon is said to have written about life in the Book of Ecclesiastes: "I have seen all the works that are done under the sun; and behold, all is vanity and vexation of spirit." To me, that passage is a caution against getting so caught up in the highs and lows of daily life on Earth that you lose sight of what should be your ultimate goal, which, as a Christian, should be to one day find happiness above the sun with God.

My earthly goal as a journalist has been to share truth by writing and editing fact-based articles, columns, and editorials that help people make up their own minds about the issues they believe are important. That was my goal even as a high school student when I was editor of the "Super Soul Special," a mimeographed newspaper for Upward Bound students at Miles College in Birmingham. Who knew that forty years later I would become the first Black editorial page editor for the *Philadelphia Inquirer*, one of America's oldest newspapers, first published in *1829*?

I didn't develop a particular writing style over those decades, but I did figure out the same approach doesn't always work to convey ideas to different readers. So, determine your audience before you write, but keep in mind that your target audience isn't the only one you must please. A reporter's preferred prose doesn't get published without first surviving a gauntlet of editors, each with his own idea of what constitutes fine writing. Newspaper editors have the power to critique your every word and to substitute their preferred verbiage at will.

Journalism professors like to stress objectivity in discussing a reporter's goal, but subjective better describes the scrutiny of an editor. Praised by one editor, a reporter's work might be deemed lackluster by another. My eventual desire to become an editor was motivated by disagreement with how some editors edited my work. But I never wanted to completely give up writing, and except for a four-year span when I was an assistant national editor at the *Inquirer* and then an assistant city editor at the *Birmingham News*, I never did.

The *Birmingham Post-Herald* first gave me a chance to both write and edit in 1979, when I was both a reporter and the Sunday city editor. That usually put me in charge of a couple of other reporters, and maybe a photographer. I also both reported and edited when I was the Alabama state news editor for United Press International from 1983 *to* 1985. I came to the *Baltimore Sun* in 1994 to be a reporter but two years later became an editorial writer. I wrote editorials and columns while serving in several editing capacities at the *Inquirer* from 1999 *to* 2018. I occasionally edited copy at the *Houston Chronicle* from 2018 *to* 2020, though my job title was senior editorial writer.

Working for five newspapers and a wire news service in four different cities, twice in Philadelphia, wasn't easy for my family. New neighbors often asked if our hopping around from city to city was because I was in the military. No, just following job opportunities, I would explain. But I did think at times that we could use the type of support that military families get to help them adjust to new surroundings. My wife was our bulwark. Each time we moved to a new city, Denice not only found a new job as a nurse but also kept our home life on an even keel.

We second-guessed some of those moves after making them—like the first time we moved to Philadelphia in 1985, only to move back to Birmingham less than two years later. We left Birmingham again in 1994 *for* my job at the *Baltimore Sun* but left there five years later when my chances for career advancement plummeted. It was back to Philadelphia to work in its South Jersey bureau, but this time we stayed nineteen years. That was the longest I held a job anywhere, but we left again after I was denied a promotion that I felt I had earned. We moved to Houston so I could work for the *Chronicle*, but after two years I decided to retire.

I was reminded of all my job moves while attending a panel discussion during the NABJ 2023 convention, which for the first time was being hosted

CHAPTER 32

by the Birmingham Association of Black Journalists, a chapter I helped found in 1983. The panelists were discussing the dwindling number of Black male journalists when a young reporter began to complain that it was not only difficult for him to support a family on his salary but frustrating that editors kept ignoring his story ideas concerning the Black community.

Several panelists suggested he might get more of the story assignments he wanted by showing his editors how well he could complete the assignments they gave him. That also might lead to better pay, they said. One panelist said the young reporter should not let his editors' lack of enthusiasm stop him from making suggestions for better coverage of the Black community. I raised my hand to agree but felt I had to also point out another truth—Black male reporters in particular must be tactful when arguing a point because too many white editors misinterpret our passion as aggression.

That doesn't mean Black reporters, male or female, should be timid. But neither should they be silenced by coworkers who want the world to believe racism doesn't exist in the supposedly liberal news media. Newsrooms aren't immune to racial prejudice. Black journalists shouldn't be afraid, but neither should they be surprised if confronted with prejudice. Instead, handle it the same way you would handle any dangerous situation—immediately and directly. Let your bosses know you won't work in that type of environment.

I don't mind admitting my prejudice. I've told white coworkers that I enter rooms expecting the white folks there to be prejudiced. That habit is common among Black folks who grew up when racism wasn't just the norm; it was the law. Even so, I always hope white people will prove me wrong. But when they don't, I don't get angry. Instead, I work even harder to dispel any notion that they are superior to me, other than their possibly higher ranking in our company's pecking order.

I think most Black people love proving white people who think they are superior wrong. We couldn't disagree more with Supreme Court Justice Clarence Thomas's assertion that affirmative action programs are confirmation that Black people need help because they are inferior. No, such programs are an acknowledgement that Black people can achieve anything when given a chance to prove our worth.

Thomas said he believes law firms questioned his intelligence when he applied for jobs because preferences based on race helped him get into Yale's law school. But he offered no proof to back up his assertion. Other Yale graduates may have gotten jobs that he didn't because of the connections their familial wealth had created. However he got into Yale, Thomas earned a law degree that opened doors for him to prove his worth. Why deny that opportunity to other Black people?

I also suggested to the young journalist during the NABJ panel discussion that he should consider working someplace else if he wasn't being paid enough to support his family, even if it meant moving to another state. I've said the same thing to other young reporters and journalism students. I was fortunate that my first job after college was in my hometown, but I left Birmingham and other cities when opportunities to learn, advance, and receive better pay developed elsewhere.

It's harder now to even threaten to leave a workplace, not just because your new job might not be any better but also because every time a Black journalist leaves a print or online publication, there is the risk that even fewer uplifting stories from the Black community they leave will be told. I talked about that in a guest commentary I was asked to contribute to—the *Inquirer*'s groundbreaking series "Black City, White Paper." Titled "When It Comes to Race, the *Inquirer* May Be Trying to Improve. But It Needs to Try Harder," this is what my commentary said:

> It has been painful to read some of the responses to the first article in The Inquirer's promised series examining how the newspaper has covered African Americans in Philadelphia, "Black City, White Paper."
>
> Painful because much of the criticism seems to dismiss the possibility that a newspaper with a clear record of promoting diversity could also be guilty of not doing as much as it could.
>
> These things are not mutually exclusive.
>
> I am a proud Inquirer alumnus, having spent more than 20 years at the paper during the '80s, '90s, and '00s, including more than a decade as editorial page editor—I was the first African American to serve in that role.
>
> During my tenure, I led many discussions with aggrieved community groups that demanded an audience with The Inquirer's leadership to complain that the paper's coverage was racially biased. This despite all of the journalism awards received by The Inquirer over the years for pointing out racial prejudice.
>
> Typically, the complainants said The Inquirer didn't interview enough or the right Black people. They criticized the paper for being

CHAPTER 32

too quick to report the bad in Black neighborhoods and too slow to report the good. That imbalance, they said, left the impression that any Black people living positive lives in Philadelphia were the exception, not the norm.

As I recall, The Inquirer news editors who participated in those conversations generally agreed that the paper's coverage wasn't perfect.

But they also pointed out the number of Black men and women holding management jobs in the newsroom, which suggested that they agreed that it was important to have that perspective in deciding what news should be covered in the Black community and who should cover it.

That's true in covering any community—be it Black, Hispanic, Asian, LGBTQ, or disabled. But acknowledging a need isn't the same as addressing it.

Because The Inquirer hasn't adequately addressed that need—as the Rev. Mark Tyler pointed out in "Black City, White Paper"—many Black Philadelphians have written it off as irrelevant.

There was a time when The Inquirer's unbalanced coverage of Black neighborhoods might have been offset to a degree by Black columnists Acel Moore and Claude Lewis, who often tried to fill in the gaps. Chuck Stone and Elmer Smith did the same thing in their columns for the Daily News. But it shouldn't be a columnist's job to compensate for a newspaper's perceived bias.

The Inquirer's financial problems since it was sold by the now-defunct Knight-Ridder news chain 15 years ago exacerbated the problem.

Genuine efforts by The Inquirer to increase diversity were all but forgotten when the paper tried to avoid going out of business by *laying off hundreds of workers*, including *Black reporters and editors*.

The perspective of those journalists has been missing from the paper ever since. So has the perspective of several of the paper's top editors who voluntarily left The Inquirer after being offered better opportunities elsewhere.

And perspective matters.

I disagree with editors who say good reporters will get the whole story no matter who they are and where they go. In the real world, a Latino reporter is likely to get better interviews in a Latino neighborhood, and a Black reporter gets better interviews in a Black neighborhood.

People feel more comfortable talking with people they identify with.

Similarly, an editor's ethnicity may help him or her see and correct mischaracterizations of a particular community before errors appear in print.

That The Inquirer has written articles and headlines that many Black people found biased doesn't mean it isn't trying to be fair; it means it needs to try harder.

The truth shouldn't be ignored, even when it hurts.

That's especially so now given the pushback against so-called "critical race theory," which seeks to erase those parts of American history that make some people feel uncomfortable about their ancestors' support of slavery and segregation.

We need to feel uncomfortable with what this country was to inspire us to work harder to make it what it should be.

Our children need to be uncomfortable with America's racist history, so they won't repeat the mistakes of the past.

So, too, should The Inquirer be uncomfortable with its past.

I owe a debt of gratitude to the paper for making me its first Black editorial page editor in 2007. In 2017, my department was reorganized, and when a managing editor of opinion position was created, I did not get the job.

Instead of keeping my office, I was given a desk in the newsroom. That was a first for an Inquirer editorial page editor. Was my treatment racist? Given similarly demeaning treatment received by other Black editors and reporters who confided in me during my 20 years at The Inquirer, I would have to say yes.

I am proud of the paper for acknowledging its past bias in "Black City, White Paper," written by Wesley Lowery, and *a subsequent apology* by Inquirer publisher Elizabeth H. Hughes.

Now it's time for those appropriate steps to be followed by corrective acts. The Inquirer should hire and promote enough Black people and other people of color to make a more discernible difference in how Philadelphia is covered.

EPILOGUE

Now that it's over, I've tried to objectively assess my forty-five years as a *newspaperman* (an archaic description of my vocation, but I like it). One recurring question I've asked myself in writing about my career is this: Did I make more mistakes than the ones I have mentioned? The answer is yes; but any regrets I have about those errors pale in comparison with the joy I felt in reporting and editing stories, editorials, and columns for United Press International, the *Birmingham Post-Herald*, *Birmingham News*, *Baltimore Sun*, *Philadelphia Inquirer*, and *Houston Chronicle*.

During my career, I met US presidents Barack Obama, George H. W. Bush, and Bill Clinton; Soviet Union president Mikhail Gorbachev; and Pakistan president Pervez Musharraf. I interviewed civil rights leaders Jesse Jackson, John Lewis, Joseph Lowery, and Fred Shuttlesworth and civil rights historians Taylor Branch, David Levering Lewis, and Wayne Flynt. I covered Birmingham's first Black mayor, Richard Arrington Jr.; Baltimore's first Black mayor, Kurt Schmoke; and Philadelphia's second Black mayor, John Street. I even got to discuss world peace with rock icon/humanitarian Bono.

More special than any of those encounters, however, were the hundreds of editorial board meetings I attended during more than forty years with people who wanted to talk about a pressing issue, request support for a worthy cause, or just have someone, anyone, listen to what they had to say.

I've met with generals, admirals, senators, governors, mayors, business executives, union bosses, pastors, rabbis, imams, community leaders, students, former prison inmates, and, most often, just plain folks. I was happy to listen to them, happy to publish what was on their minds, and even happier when I could add my two cents to the conversation.

That's the type of interaction that helped newspapers gain their reputation as the fourth "estate" or branch of government. When a newspaper publishes articles and fact-based editorials that report what self-interested politicians and corporations don't want people to know, the public is then armed with the ammunition it needs to demand justice.

Unfortunately, that interaction has become increasingly rare, as editorial pages continue to be eliminated. It's not that these often one- or two-person departments are too expensive to operate. But they can be costly in other ways, including losing advertising revenue when an editorial or commentary offends the wrong person or company—not to mention the potential cost of litigation. As the *Inquirer* changed ownership multiple times, it cut ties with its longtime legal counsel to avoid paying attorneys' fees and settled a scurrilous libel lawsuit that was filed by a congressman against the editorial board when I led it.

There's no dearth of opinions in the current digital age of journalism, but too many of them are far from being fact-based. Too many web publications spew dubious commentaries aimed at increasing their digital audiences and advertising revenue without allowing facts to get in the way.

There's no going backward. Digital journalism isn't the future; it's now! And print newspapers will continue to die. That doesn't make me sad. I'm grateful for the forty-five years during which I got to work for some outstanding publications. I'm also hopeful that journalism will eventually catch up with technology and find a way to both pay the bills and serve an audience that still wants the unvarnished truth.

INDEX

Page numbers in italics refer to photographs.

abortion, 134–37
Abron, Charles, 17, 34, 39, 42, 73
academic achievement, Jackson's, 12, 13, 14. *See also* education
accent, Jackson's, 9, 74
Adams, Oscar Sr., 52
Addis Ababa, 126–27
adversity, overcoming, 35
affirmative action programs, 150–51
African American History Month, 143. *See also* history, Black
AIDS/HIV, 1, 98, 109–10. *See also* homosexuality; Jackson, Calvin
Alabama, University of, ix, 36–37, 95
Alabama Christian Movement for Human Rights, 16
Alabama Press Association, 58
Alabama Scholastic Press Association (ASPA), 95
alcohol, 53–55, 60–63
Alpha Kappa Alpha, 85
Alvarez, Rafael, 97
Amos 'n' Andy (television series), 8
Annie Allen (Brooks), 93
appearance, 13, 31, 55–56
armed forces, desegregation/integration of, 144
Arrington, Richard, Jr., 77, 99, 141, 154
Ashe, Arthur, 98

Asher, Jim, 100
ASPA (Alabama Scholastic Press Association), 95
Associated Press, 80
Atkinson, Clettus, 53
Atlanta, 41
awards, Jackson's: Alabama Press Association's "best editorial," 58; from Associated Press, 57; Pulitzer Prize (1991), 69, 88–92; Southern Horizons award, 37

Baker University, 9, 42; Black student union (BSU; Mungano), 43–44; civil rights and, 44; journalism at, 45; paying for, 45, 46; photograph of, *68*; social life at, 44–45
Baldwin Methodist Church, 44
Baltimore, 96, 97, 99, 154
Baltimore Evening Sun, 98, 100
Baltimore Sun, 154; Black journalists at, 95–96, 97, 99, 111–12, 149; editorial board, 100, 112; Jackson as reporter for, 97; Jackson assigned to city hall, 99; Jackson offered job at, 95–96; Jackson's career at, 149; Jackson's friends/social life at, 97, 111; "The Secrets That We Keep," 110; staff members, 97, 99; Thomas at, 111–12. *See also* Marimow, Bill

157

INDEX

Banisky, Sandy, 97
Baptists, 6
Barnes, Bob, 60–61
Baye, Betty, 98
Beene, Rick, 78, 79
Bell, Esther, 28
Bell, Luther, 28
Bennett, Allegra, 98
Beyerle, Dana, 80
Birmingham: Jackson's moves to, 84–85, 149; medical industry in, 77–78. *See also* segregation
Birmingham Association of Black Journalists, 83, 150
Birmingham News, 154; Black journalists with, 52, 85, 86; "Bubba Has Brain" editorial, 58; career advancement at, 94–95; editorial board, 85–86, 88–89, 94; Jackson hired by, 85; Jackson's interview with, 50–51; school funding editorial series, 94; tax reform editorial series, 94; "Torn Lampshade" award, 85; transition to digital-only, 138
Birmingham Post-Herald, 154; Black journalists with, 52, 61–62; closure of, 138; coverage of police brutality protest, 68; friends from, 73–74; Jackson's career at, 149; Jackson's friendships/lifestyle at, 53–55, 60–63, 64; Jackson's interview with, 51; Jackson's reassignment at, 77; McEachran at, 77; newsroom management job, 57; pay at, 78, 79; staff members, 52, 53–55, 56, 61–62. *See also* LeGrand, Duard
Birmingham Times, 41
Birmingham World, 41, 86
Birmingham Youth Presbytery, 24–25
Bissinger, H. G. "Buzz," 120, 122
"Black," meaning of, 142
"Black City, White Paper" series (*Philadelphia Inquirer*), 151–53

Black Enterprise (magazine), 99
Black Panthers, 43
Black people: double lives of, x, 9, 44, 74; interactions with white people, 150; newspapers' coverage of, 52, 152; oppression and, 142; perceived as aggressive, 150; in prison, 146. *See also* desegregation/integration; journalists, Black; justice; men, Black; racism; segregation
Black student union (BSU; Mungano), 43–44
Blakely, Nora, 93
Blalock, Bob, 85, 92
Blissett, Elisha, 13
"Bloody Sunday" marchers, 86–87
"Bombingham," 21
bombings, 19–24, 47
Bono, 154
Boston Globe, 98
Boutwell Auditorium, 62
Bowden, Mark, 120, 122
Bragg, Rick, 85
Branch, Taylor, 154
bribes, 21–23
Brick Yard. *See* Loveman Village
Brooks, Gwendolyn, 93
Brown, Mattie, 32
Brown, Michael, 145
Brown v. Board of Education, 16, 36. *See also* desegregation/integration
Bryant, Paul "Bear," 80, 119
Bryant, Ted, 51
Bryant, W. Arnett, 52
"Bubba Has Brain" (editorial; Jackson), 58
bullies, 10, 17–18
Burney, Melanie, 121–22
Burton, Cindy, 121–22
Busby, Julie, 112
Bush, George H. W., 154
Bush, George W., 136

Campbell, Sylvester, 33

INDEX

Cannon, Joe, 61
Cannon, Terry, 61
capitalism, 128, 129
career, Jackson's: Black mayors and, 154; desire for advancement opportunities, 94–95; editorial boards and, 86, 148, 154; Jackson's goal in, 148; Jackson's reflections on, 148–55; moves and, 149–50, 151; newspapers worked at during, 154; people encountered during, 154; racism and, 150–53; retirement, 139. *See also* Jackson, Harold; journalism; journalists, Black; *individual newspapers*
Carter, Clyde, 6
Carter, Wyoming, 97
Casey, Ron, *69*, 86, 94
cemeteries, 26, 119
Center Street Elementary School, 12–14
challenges, need for preparation, 18
Chamberlain, Charles "Chas," 80
Chambliss, Robert "Dynamite Bob," 22
charity, 30–32
Chavis, Benjamin F., Jr., 78
"Cheap Date, The" (editorial; Jackson), 89–92
Chengwei Capital, 128
Cherry, Bobby Frank, 22
children, racism and, 15–24
China, 127–29
Christian and Missionary Alliance, 133–37
Christian belief, Jackson's, 119. *See also* churches; religion
churches: decline in attendance, 32; desegregation and, 24–25; 16th Street Baptist Church, 20–24, 47; Sixth Avenue Baptist Church, 35; in South Jersey, 133–37; Westminster Presbyterian Church, 5–7, 24–25, 32, 118–19. *See also* religion; *individual denominations*
Church of Christ, 133

Civil Rights Act (1964), 24, 144. *See also* civil rights movement
civil rights movement: Black newspapers and, 86; bombings, 19–24, 47; children and, 16–24; Civil Rights Act (1964), 24, 144; defense of homes during, 24; education and, 43; Gaston and, 98–99, 137; Emory O. Jackson and, 41–42, 86; Coretta Scott King, 141; Martin Luther King Jr., 16, 19, 98, 145; Selma to Montgomery march, 86–87; Shuttlesworth, 16, 154; Upward Bound, 42–44, 148; violence against journalists during, 55; Voting Rights Act (1965), 24, 144. *See also* desegregation/integration
civil unions, 135. *See also* homosexuality
Civil War, 8–9, 144–45
Clemon, U. W., 78
Clinton, Bill, 154
Clinton, Hillary, 136, 141
clothing, 31, 55–56
Coca-Cola USA, 41, 86
Cohen, Jeff, 138
Coleman, Reva, 36
college: applying for, 43; desegregation and, 36–37; graduation from, 50; HBCUs, 42–44, 148; journalism scholarship, 41, 86; paying for, 45, 46. *See also* Baker University; education
Collins, Addie Mae, 20
columnists, Black. *See* career, Jackson's; editorial boards; journalists, Black
communism, 128, 129
Confederate traitors, statues of, 8–9, 144
Connor, Eugene "Bull," 16, 55
Cooke, Russell, 121
Cooper, Connie, 9
Cooper, June, 9
Corlew, Carole, 78
Corner, The (Simon), 97
corporal punishment, 10–11
corruption, 21–23

159

INDEX

Crenshaw, Solomon, 85
criminality, 146. *See also* justice
"critical race theory," 143, 153. *See also* history, Black
Cullum, Mark, 86
Curry, George, 121, 122

"Daddy." *See* Jackson, Lewis
Daemmrich, JoAnna, 99
Daily News. See *Philadelphia Daily News*
Da Ping, 71, 128, 129
Davies, Paul, 121, 122
Davis, Jefferson, 144
Dear Denise (McNair), 22
debating, 10
Delaney, Paul, 95
democracy, 127, 128, 155
Democratic Party, 134. *See also* abortion; Obama, Barack; politics
desegregation/integration: of armed forces, 144; bars/musical venues and, 61; churches and, 24–25; education and, 14, 39–41; experiences with white people and, ix–x, 37, 39–41, 44; Loveman Village and, 39; of University of Alabama, 36–37. *See also* civil rights movement
discipline, 5, 10–11, 18, 31
domestic violence, 60
double lives, Black people's, x, 9, 44, 74
Down Home (magazine), 21
Downing, Annye, 32
drug dealers, reporters and, 97
Du Bois, W. E. B., x, 9, 44, 74
Dubose, Lonzo, 115
Dubose, Sara Jane Jones, 115

earmarking, 89
Ebonics, 74
editorial boards: *Baltimore Evening Sun*, 100; *Baltimore Sun*, 100, 112; *Birmingham News*, 85–86, 88–89, 94; Jackson and, 86, 148, 154; *Philadelphia Daily News*, 131; *Philadelphia Inquirer*, 113, 120–24, 131, 148. *See also* career, Jackson's; journalists, Black
editorial pages, elimination of, 155
editors, 148–49
Edmund Pettus Bridge, 86–87
education: affirmative action programs, 150–51; Black teachers, 35, 36; Center Street Elementary School, 12–14; civil rights movement and, 43; desegregation and, 14, 36–37, 39–41; HBCUs, 42–44, 148; high schools, 6, 13, 33–34, 39–41; journalism scholarship, 41, 86; journalism workshop, ix, 36, 37; parent-teacher meetings, 31; paying for, 45, 46; reading, 5, 12; school funding editorial series, 94; "separate but equal," 16; underemployment of Black men and, 21; Upward Bound, 42–44, 148. *See also* academic achievement, Jackson's; Alabama, University of; Baker University; college
Ellis, Glenn, 20
Emerge (magazine), 121
Estes, Jim, 133
Estes, Judy, 133
Ethiopia, 71, 125–27
Eubanks, Curtis, 57
evangelism, 134, 136
Evening Sun. See *Baltimore Evening Sun*
Extraordinary, Ordinary People (Rice), 6

fairness, 145–47. *See also* justice
Falkenberg, Lisa, 139
Family Research Council, 136
Ferris, Kevin, 121
Fisher, Ricky, 44
Fletcher, Mike, 99
flu pandemic, 115
Flynt, Wayne, 154
food, 115–16

INDEX

Ford, Abiyi, 127
Ford, Bessie, 80, 124
Fortune, Clarence, 31
Foster, Autherine Lucy, 36–37
Franck, Kurt, 79
Freedom Forum, 95
Freedom Riders, 55
Freedom's Children (Levin), 16
freelance budgets, 120–21, 122
Friedman, Sally, 113
Frierson, Clara, 13
future, outside of housing projects, 4
Fu Ying, 128

games, 5
Garner, Ed, 16
Garner, Eric, 145
Garrison, Greg, 85
Gaston, A. G., 98–99, 137
Gaston Motel, 19
Gates, Steve, 60
gay men, treatment of, 63–64. *See also* homosexuality; Jackson, Calvin
gay rights, 134, 135. *See also* homosexuality; Jackson, Calvin
Gee's Bend quilts, 100
Gibson, Heywood, 33
Giovanni, Nikki, 43
Glover, Evelyn, 32
Gohlke, Josh, *70*, 124
Goings, Martha Henderson, 28
Goode, Wilson, 141
Gorbachev, Mikhail, 154
government, 58. *See also* politics
Grace Hill Cemetery, 26, 119
Grateful Dead, 62
Gray Ghost, The (television series), 8
Greek organizations, 44
Gregory, Dick, 44

Hall, Bob, 123, 131
Hall, Wiley, 98
Halsey, Ashley, 81

Hamilton, Harold, 41
"Handcuffing Money" (editorial; Jackson), 89
Hansen, Jeff, 85, 92
Hanson, Victor II, 86
Hardy, Jeff, 60, 61–62
Harris, Mabel Jean, *66*
Harris, Mark, 80
Harris, Mike, 53–54, 60, 61
Hay, Tom, 25
HBCUs (historically Black colleges and universities), 42–44, 148
Healing the Children, 125–26
HealthSouth, 23
Hearst Corporation, 139
hedge funds, 121
Heflin, Howell, 78
help, asking for, 35
Henderson, Harold M., 28
Henderson, Randy, 85
Hendricks, Audrey Faye, 16
High, Johnnie Mae, 14
high schools, 6, 13, 33–34, 39–41. *See also* education
Hill, Miriam G., 38
Hill, Thomas, 33
historically Black colleges and universities (HBCUs), 42–44, 148
history, American. *See* statues, of Confederate traitors
history, Black, 98–99, 143–45, 153. *See also* statues, of Confederate traitors
"hitting back," 18
HIV/AIDS, 1, 98, 109–10. *See also* homosexuality; Jackson, Calvin
Holmes, Groove, 62
Holt, Dennis, 55
Homicide (Simon), 97
homosexuality: as crime, 63; religion and, 135–36; truth and, 2, 11; views of, 63–64, 110. *See also* AIDS/HIV; Jackson, Calvin
Hood, James, 36

161

INDEX

hooks, bell, 43
Horn, Frank, 4–5, 146
Horne, Gail, 40, 41
Horvath, Karen, 45
housing projects, 4. *See also* Loveman Village
Houston, Texas, 138–40, 149
Houston Chronicle, 138–40, 149, 154
Huawei Technologies, 128
Hughes, Elizabeth H., 153
human papillomavirus, 126

IGM (Interstate General Media), 123. *See also* Lenfest, H. G. "Gerry"
Ingram, Bill, 55
Inky. See *Philadelphia Inquirer*
integration. *See* civil rights movement; desegregation/integration; education
International Typographical Union (ITU), 79
Interstate General Media (IGM), 123
interviews, 55, 56
ITU (International Typographical Union), 79

Jackson, Annette, 78
Jackson, Anthony (Skippy), 3, 6, 30; birth of, 29; death of, 103; photograph of, *67*; respect for, 33
Jackson, Berry, 27
Jackson, Calvin, 1–2; birth of, 29; Christmas in Baltimore, 101–2; at college, 59; death of, 109; fears for, 63–64; Anthony Jackson's funeral and, 103; Harold Jackson's column about, 109–10; Harold Jackson's relationship with, 63, 101; Harold Jackson's visit to, 109; at Harold Jackson's wedding, 75; Janye Jackson and, 63, 104; news of impending death, 1, 100, 103; partner of, 104–8, 135; personality of, 10–11, 34; photograph of, *67*; in San Francisco, 64; toys and, 5; truth and, 3, 11

Jackson, Denice, 64; career of, 84, 85; education of, 50; Jackson's meeting of, 44; photograph of, *71*; proposal/wedding, 73–76
Jackson, Dennis, 78
Jackson, Derrick Z., 98
Jackson, Don, 3, 17, 96–97; birth of, 29; character of, 34; photograph of, *66, 67*
Jackson, Emory O., 41–42, 86
Jackson, Harold: birth of, 29; children of, 78; grandchildren of, 114, 119; grandparents of, 27–28; photographs of, *66, 67, 68, 69, 70, 71, 72*
Jackson, Janye: background of, 114–17; culinary skills of, 115–16; death of, 114, 117–18; discipline and, 5; first husband, 117; funeral of, 118–19; grandparents of, 115; great-granddaughters of, 119; health of, 84; Calvin Jackson and, 63, 107; Harold Jackson's marriage and, 75; Lewis Jackson and, 117; Lewis Jackson's death and, 30–32; marriage of, 28–29; move to Baltimore, 96; parents of, 114–15; photographs of, *65, 67*; pride of, 31; religion and, 6; reputation of, in Loveman Village, 59–60; Westminster Presbyterian Church and, 32, 118–19; work done by, 31
Jackson, Jefferson, 27
Jackson, Jeffery, 3; birth of, 29; character of, 40; photograph of, *67*
Jackson, Jesse, 141, 154
Jackson, Lewis, 117; ancestry of, 27–28; character of, 27; death of, 26; discipline and, 5; Janye Jackson and, 117; jobs of, 29; life of, 27–29; photograph of, *65*; religion and, 6–7
Jackson, Margaret, 27
Jackson, Rebecca, 27–28
Jackson, Shandra, 13, 41
Jacobson, Jim, 50, 85, 86

INDEX

Jenkins, Phil, 80
job experience, Jackson's: *Birmingham Post-Herald* interview and, 50–51; during college, 45, 47–49. *See also* career, Jackson's
Johnson, Bob, 53
Jones, Lula Mae, 114
Jones, Sara Jane, 115
Jones, Sheinelle, 21
Jones, Vivian Malone, 36
journalism: at Baker, 45; editors, 148–49; Jackson's early experience in, 50–51; Jackson's introduction to, ix, 36; stereotypes and, 38. *See also* career, Jackson's; journalists, Black
journalism, digital, 121, 123, 130–31, 138, 155
journalism, print, 130, 138, 139. *See also* newspapers
journalism workshop (University of Alabama), ix, 36, 37
journalists, Black, 150–53; appearance of, 55–56; at *Baltimore Evening Sun*, 98; at *Baltimore Sun*, 95–96, 97, 99, 111–12, 149; Birmingham Association of Black Journalists, 83, 150; at *Birmingham News*, 52, 85, 86; at *Birmingham Post-Herald*, 52, 61–62; Black mayors and, 77; Black newspapers, 41, 86; at *Boston Globe*, 98; constraints placed on, 98; at *Louisville Courier-Journal*, 98; NABJ, 20, 22, 83, 95, 98, 149–50, 151; at *Philadelphia Daily News*, 152; at *Philadelphia Inquirer*, 98, 120–25, 148, 152; public's reluctance to speak to, 55–56; at *Rochester Democrat and Chronicle*, 98; at *Tennessean* (Nashville), 98; "Thinking Black" essay collection, 98–99; at *Washington Times*, 98. *See also* editorial boards; *individual journalists*; *individual papers*

Junck, Mary E., 111
justice, 21–23, 51–52, 142, 145–46, 155

Katz, Lewis, 123, 130
Kestenbaum, Herb, 81
Keyes, Alan, 135
Kindred, Ingrid, 85
King, A. D., 19
King, B. B., 62
King, Coretta Scott, 141
King, Martin Luther, Jr., 16, 19, 98, 145
Martin Luther King Jr. Day, 145
Knight Ridder chain, 120
Ku Klux Klan, 19, 20, 21, 47, 55

Lake, Richard (Mafundi), 56–57
Langford, Larry, 23, *68*
Langston, Tommy, 55
LaPierre, Al, 23
Lard, Eddie, 85
Last Poets, 43
Lawrence, Kathy, 95
lawsuits, 132
Ledford, Joey, *69*, 80
LeGrand, Duard, 51, 52, 56, 77. *See also Birmingham Post-Herald*
Lenfest, H. G. "Gerry," 123
Lenfest Institute, 130
LeVert, Henry, 30
Levin, Ellen, 16
Lewis, Claude, 98, 152
Lewis, David Levering, 154
Lewis, Dwight, 98
Lewis, Jezeree, 14
Lewis, John, 87, 154
Li, Eric X., 128
library, 5
Lid Law, 90
Lindeborg, Richard, 45
Lippman, Laura, 97
Lippman, Theo, Jr., 97
Loeb, Vernon, 138

163

INDEX

Louisville Courier-Journal, Black journalists at, 98
Loveman's (department store), 19
Loveman Village, 3–5; during civil rights movement, 24; conditions in, 60–61; desegregation and, 39; Harold Jackson's illegal residency in, 59; Janye Jackson's reputation in, 59–60; photograph of, *66*; playing outdoors in, 9–10; violence and, 33
Lowery, Joseph, 154
Lowery, Wesley, 153
Lowry, Bob, 80
Loyola College of Maryland, 98

Mafundi (Richard Lake), 56–57
"Mama." *See* Jackson, Janye
"Mama Jack," 27–28
Mangels, John, 85
Marimow, Bill, 95, 98, 99, 100. See also *Baltimore Sun*
Marquis, Ricky, 1, 103, 107
marriage, Jackson's, 64. *See also* Jackson, Denice
marriage, same-sex, 135–36. *See also* homosexuality
mayors, Black: Arrington, 77, 99, 141, 154; Black journalists' coverage of, 77; Goode, 141; Langford, 23, *68*; Schmoke, 99, 154; Street, 154; Young, 141. *See also* politics
Mays, Clarence (Bud), 44, 45
Mazurek, Pat, 121
McClatchy chain, 120
McCraven, Marilyn, 112
McDougal, Billy, 78
McEachran, Angus, 77
McNair, Chris, 21–23
McNair, Denise, 20, 21, 22
McNair, Lisa, 22
McNair, Maxine, 21
Medders, Orbie, 79

media, 7–8. *See also* journalism; newspapers; television
medical industry, 77–78
men, Black: underemployment of, 21; work of, 131
Meng Wanzhou, 128
"Message to Black Men, A" (essay; Jackson), 98–99
Methodists, 44
Miles College, 42–44, 148
Miller, Doug, 139
Mintz, Evan, 139
Mitchell, Gary, 61
Moore, Acel, 83, 152
Moore, Geraldine, 52
Morring, Frank, 53, 60, 73–74
Mosby, John Singleton, 8
moves, in Jackson's career, 149–50, 151
Mullins, Ed, 95
Mungano (Black student union), 43–44
Murray, Cecil L., 44
Murray, Robert, 62–63
Musharraf, Pervez, 154

NAACP, 43, 78
National Association of Black Journalists (NABJ), 20, 22, 83, 95, 98, 149–50, 151
National Newspaper Publishers Association (NNPA), 41, 86
Naughton, Jim, 81
Negro History Week, 143. *See also* history, Black
Nesbitt, Jim, 60
Newkirk, Jim, 139
"New South," 61. *See also* desegregation/integration
news outlets, digital, 121, 123, 130–31, 138, 155
newspaper columnists, Black. *See* journalists, Black
Newspaper Guild, 79
"newspaperman," 154. *See also* career,

Jackson's; editorial boards; Jackson, Harold; journalists, Black
newspapers: coverage of Black community by, 52, 152; decline of, 121, 130, 138, 139, 155; editorial pages eliminated by, 155; importance of, 155; staff/budget cuts, 121–25, 152. *See also* journalists, Black; *individual papers*
newspapers, Black, 41, 86. *See also individual papers*
New York Times, 95, 143
"Nickels and Dimes" (editorial; Jackson), 89
NNPA (National Newspaper Publishers Association), 41, 86
Norcross, George E., III, 123, 130
Norris, Clarence, 52
nursing homes, 118

Obama, Barack, 22, *72*, 134, 136, 141–43, 154
objectivity, 149
Olesker, Michael, 97
Ollove, Mike, 97
online news outlets, 121, 123, 130–31, 138, 155
oppression, Blackness and, 142
Osberg, Greg, 122, 131

parent-teacher meetings, 31
Parker High School, 39
Parsons, James, 56
parties, 44
Partners in Neighborhood Growth (PING), 4
patriotism, Jackson's, 145
Paulson, Beverly, 45
Payne, James, 40
performers, Black, 7
Peter (Calvin's partner), 104–8, 135
Pettus, James, 33
Philadelphia, 81–82, 83, 149

Philadelphia Daily News, 120; Black journalists at, 152; editorial board, 131; loss of revenue, 121; ownership of, 123, 130–31; strike at, 84
Philadelphia Inquirer, 154; "Black City, White Paper" series, 151–53; Black journalists at, 98, 120–25, 148, 152; editorial board, 113, 120–24, 131, 148; financial problems, 121, 152; freelance budget, 121, 122; Jackson's affection for, 132; Jackson's application to, 80; Jackson's career at, 149; *New York Times* on, 143; Obama and, 141–43; op-ed page, 123–24; ownership of, 123, 130–31; politics and, 141–43; retribution against Jackson, 123–24, 131; South Jersey newsroom, 112; staff/budget cuts, 121–25, 152; strike at, 84; "When Faith and Politics Overlap," 135
Philadelphia Media Holdings (PMH), 120
Philadelphia Media Network, 121
Philly.com, 121, 123, 130–31
photographers, 55
Pietila, Antero, 100
Pietila, Barbara, 100
Pizitz, 19
Pledger, Brenda, 44
Pledger, Denice, 44. *See also* Jackson, Denice
PMH (Philadelphia Media Holdings), 120
poetry, written by Jackson, 74–75
police, Birmingham, 145–46; Black, 4–5, 146; Connor, 16; Horn, 4–5, 146; Jackson's reluctance to interview, 55, 56; violence of against Black children, 24, 145
police brutality, 24, *68*, 86–87, 145–46
politics: abortion, 134–37; bribery/corruption in, 21–23; "Bubba Has Brain" editorial, 58; in China, 127–29;

INDEX

Democratic Party, 134; elimination of editorial pages and, 155; in Ethiopia, 126–27; freelance contracts and, 120–21; gay rights and, 134, 135–36; Jackson's writings about, 141–47; newspapers' importance and, 155; Obama, 22, 72, 134, 136, 141–43, 154; *Philadelphia Inquirer* and, 141–43; religion and, 135; Republican Party, 136; taxes, 88–92, 94; Trump, 136, 137; war on terror, 126–27. *See also* government; mayors, Black
pollution, 129
poverty, 30–32, 129, 147
prejudice, 150. *See also* racism
preparation, challenges and, 18
Presbyterians, 24–25, 133. *See also* Westminster Presbyterian Church
Price, Jeff, 80
pride, 31
Prince, Richard, 98
prison, 146. *See also* justice
professor, Jackson as, 95, 98
property tax system, 89
Pulitzer Prize winners: *Birmingham News* (Jackson, Casey, and Ledford), 69, 88–92; Bragg, 85; Brooks, 93; Falkenberg, 139; Marimow, 95; Moore, 83; school funding editorial series as finalist, 94; seventy-fifth anniversary celebration of, 92–93. *See also* awards, Jackson's

quilts, 100

racism: appearance and, 13; children and, 15–24; Gaston and, 137; Jackson's career and, 150–53; in journalism, 150–53; religion and, 25; underemployment of Black men and, 21
Ramsay High School, 39–41
rap music, 8
Rascovar, Barry, 111

Rassenfoss, Joe, 60, 61–62
reading, 5, 12
Redding, Otis, 98
religion: Baker University and, 44; Birmingham Youth Presbytery, 24–25; evangelism, 134, 136; homosexuality and, 134, 135–36; Denice Jackson and, 133; Harold Jackson and, 133; Janye Jackson and, 6; Lewis Jackson and, 6–7; politics and, 135; poverty and, 147; racism and, 25; Westminster Presbyterian Church, 5–7, 24–25, 32, 118–19; Wright, 142. *See also* churches; *individual denominations*
reporters, Black. *See* career, Jackson's; journalists, Black
Republican Party, 136. *See also* politics
respect, mutual, 124
Rice, Condoleezza, 6
Rice, John, 6
Ritchey, Michael, 125–26
Robertson, Carole, 20
Robinson, Johnny, 24
Robinson, Kathryn, 36
Rochester Democrat and Chronicle, Black columnists with, 98
role models, 4–5
Rubin, Trudy, 121, 124
Rudolph, George, 20
Rudolph, Sarah Collins, 20, 22

Santorum, Rick, 120, 122
Satullo, Chris, 113, 120
Scarritt, Tom, 86
Schaffer, Jan, 81
Schmoke, Kurt, 99, 154
scholarship, journalism, 41, 86
schools. *See* education
Scott-Heron, Gil, 43
Scottsboro Boys, 51–52
Sears, Jackson's job at, 48–49
secrets, 119. *See also* Jackson, Calvin

INDEX

"Secrets That We Keep, The" (column; Jackson), 110
segregation, ix; adults and, 15, 21; in Birmingham, 5; Black teachers during, 35; children sheltered by, 15; "separate but equal," 16; Wallace and, 36, 47. *See also* civil rights movement; desegregation/integration; racism
Selma to Montgomery march, 86–87
"separate but equal," 16
Shea, Sandy, 131–32
Sheehy, Roscoe, 12–13
Shores, Arthur, 19
Shuttlesworth, Fred, 16, 154
Siegel, Eric, 99
Siegelman, Don, 23
Simon, David, 97
16th Street Baptist Church, 20–24, 47
Sixth Avenue Baptist Church, 35
"Skippy." *See* Jackson, Anthony (Skippy)
slaves, in Jackson's ancestry, 27
Smith, Elmer, 152
Smith, Julia Emma, 6
Snoddy, John, 57–58
Southern Christian Leadership Conference, 43
Southern Horizons award, 37
South Jersey, 112, 133–37. *See also Philadelphia Inquirer*
Spain Rehabilitation Hospital, 47–48
speech, Jackson's, 9, 74
Spielman, J. Ward (Sparky), 46
spirituality, 6. *See also* religion; Westminster Presbyterian Church
sports, coverage of, 80
Sprague, Dick, 132
Springer, Alicia, 13
Springer, John, 13
Stansel, Mary E., 78
statues, of Confederate traitors, 8–9, 144
stereotypes, 7–8, 38
Sterling, Laura P., 12, 14
Sterne, Joseph R. L., 100, 111

Stevens, Carol, 112
Steverson, Bill, 53
Stewart, Sherrel Wheeler, 85
Stone, Chuck, 152
Stouppe, Hugh, 43
Street, John, 154
Student Nonviolent Coordinating Committee, 43, 87
subjectivity, 149
Suh, Il Roh, 45
Swain, Theodore Roosevelt, 57
Sweeney, Pat, 121

taxes, 88–92, 94. *See also* politics
Taylor, David, 81
teachers, Black, 35, 36
Teamsters Union, 82
television, 5, 7–9, 28
Tennessean (Nashville), 98
Tenodros, Solomon, 126
"Thinking Black" (essay collection), 98–99
Thomas, Clarence, 121, 150–51
Thomas, Hannah, 116
Thomas, Jacqueline, 111–12
Thomas, Lee, 116
Thomas, Mary, 117
Thomas, Mullie, 116
Thomas, Sid, 56–57
Tierney, Brian, 120, 122, 141, 143
Titusville community, 5, 28, 117
Todd, Senora, 9
tornadoes, 57, 97
"Torn Lampshade" award, 85
Tortorano, David, 80
toys, 5
travel: to China, 127–29; to Ethiopia, 125–27
Trinity Christian Chapel, 133–37
Truman, Harry S., 144
Trump, Donald, 58, 136, 137
truth, 2, 11
Turner, Nathan, 85

167

INDEX

Tyler, Mark, 152

UAB hospital, 78
Ullman High School, 6, 13, 33, 36, 39. *See also* education
unions, 79, 81, 82, 84
United Press International (UPI), 37, 51–52, 78–80, 81, 124, 149, 154
University of Alabama. *See* Alabama, University of
UPI (United Press International), 37, 51–52, 78–80, 81, 124, 149, 154
Upward Bound, 42–44, 148

Vanhorn, Alvin, 10
Veteran's Hospital, Jackson's job at, 49
violence: bullies and, 10, 17–18; on Edmund Pettus Bridge, 86–87; high school and, 33–34; against journalists, 55; Loveman Village and, 33; police brutality, 24, 86–87, 145–46
Virgil, 119
voters, Southern, 58
Voting Rights Act (1965), 24, 144. *See also* civil rights movement

Walking With the Wind (Lewis), 87
Wallace, George, ix, 36, 47–48, 52
Ware, Jim, 55
Ware, Virgil, 24
Wark, Lois, 81, 83
war on terror, 126–27
Washington Times, Black columnists with, 98
Weaver, Emmett, 62

websites. *See* journalism, digital
Welch, Adrienne, 52
Wesley, Cynthia, 20
West, Norris, 112
Westminster Presbyterian Church, 5–7, 24–25, 32, 118–19
"What They Won't Tell You about Your Taxes" (editorials; *Birmingham News*), 88–89
"When Faith and Politics Overlap" (editorial; Jackson), 135
"When It Comes to Race, the *Inquirer* May Be Trying to Improve. But It Needs to Try Harder" (column; Jackson), 151–53
White, Andrea, 139
White, Gregory Durr, 35
Whitehead, Lorenzo, 117
white people, experiences with, ix–x, 37, 39–41, 44. *See also* Baker University; desegregation/integration; journalism workshop
Wickham, DeWayne, 98
Wilson, Ace, 114–15
Wilson, Janye Lee. *See* Jackson, Janye
Wischnowski, Stan, 121, 122, 131
Wolf Call (student newspaper), 36
Woodard, Jeff, 80
Woodson, Carter G., 143
work, of Black men, 21, 131
Wright, Jeremiah A., 142

Yoo, John, 120–21, 122
Young, Andrew, 141